Discovering Dinosaurs

HORNED, SPIKED, AND CRESTED DINOSAURS

Consulting Editor: Carl Mehling

Skyview Books
an imprint of
WINDMILL BOOKS
New York

Published in 2010 by Windmill Books, LLC
303 Park Avenue South, Suite # 1280, New York, NY 10010-3657

CREDITS:
Consulting Editor: Carl Mehling
Designer: Graham Beehag

Publisher Cataloging in Publication

Horned, spiked, and crested dinosaurs / consulting editor, Carl Mehling.
p. cm. – (Discovering dinosaurs)
Summary: With the help of fossil evidence this book provides physical descriptions of twenty-nine dinosaurs with horns, spikes or crests.—Contents: Megapnosaurus—Cryolophosaurus—Dilophosaurus—Metriacanthosaurus—Ceratosaurus—Chialingosaurus—Ouranosaurus—Spinosaurus—Anchiceratops—Arrhinoceratops—Bagaceratops—Brachylophosaurus—Chasmosaurus—Chirostenotes—Corythosaurus—Diceratus—Einiosaurus—Hypacrosaurus—Jaxartosaurus—Microceratops—Montanoceratops—Nipponosaurus—Pachyrhinosaurus—Pentaceratops—Prosaurolophus—Parasaurolophus—Protoceratops—Triceratops—Styracosaurus.
ISBN 978-1-60754-775-4. – ISBN 978-1-60754-783-9 (pbk.)
ISBN 978-1-60754-857-7 (6-pack)
1. Dinosaurs—Juvenile literature [1. Dinosaurs] I. Mehling, Carl
II. Series
567.9—dc22

Printed in the United States

CPSIA Compliance Information: Batch #BW10W: For further information contact Windmill Books, New York, New York at 1-866-478-0556.

CONTENTS

Introduction

Imagining what our world was like in the distant past is a lot like being a detective. There were no cameras around, and there were no humans writing history books. In many cases, fossils are all that remain of animals who have been extinct for millions of years.

Fossils are the starting point that scientists use to make educated guesses about what life was like in prehistoric times. And while fossils are important, even the best fossil can't tell the whole story. If snakes were extinct, and all we had left were their bones, would anyone guess that they could snatch bats from the air in pitch-black caves? Probably not, but there is a Cuban species of snake that can do just that. Looking at a human skeleton wouldn't tell you how many friends that person had, or what their favorite color was. Likewise, fossils can give us an idea of how an animal moved and what kind of food it ate, but they can't tell us everything about an animal's behavior or what life was like for them.

Our knowledge of prehistoric life is constantly changing to fit the new evidence we have. While we may never know everything, the important thing is that we continue to learn and discover. Learning about the history of life on Earth, and trying to piece together the puzzle of the dinosaurs, can help us understand more about our past and future.

Megapnosaurus

• **ORDER** • Saurischia • **FAMILY** • Coelophysoidea
• **GENUS & SPECIES** • *Megapnosaurus rhodesiensis, M. kayentakatae*

VITAL STATISTICS

Fossil Location	Africa, North America
Diet	Carnivorous
Pronunciation	me-gap-no-SAWR-us
Weight	66 lbs (30 kg)
Length	10 ft (3 m)
Height	32 in (80 cm)
Meaning of Name	"Big dead lizard"

FOSSIL EVIDENCE

Light, hollow bones and long, powerful legs made *Megapnosaurus* a swift bipedal runner. It may have hunted in packs, possibly chasing small mammals and lizards. Discovery of *Megapnosaurus* in both Africa and North America suggests that it migrated across the continents when they were joined as the one supercontinent called Pangaea. Differences in the North American and African fossils show how the species adapted (changed) to fit their different environments.

This athletic, lightweight dinosaur hunted small prey in packs. It was called *Syntarsus* until scientists discovered that the name was already assigned to a beetle.

Crest
Unlike the African species, which had no crest, the American species of *Megapnosaurus* had a double crest on top of its head.

WHERE IN THE WORLD?

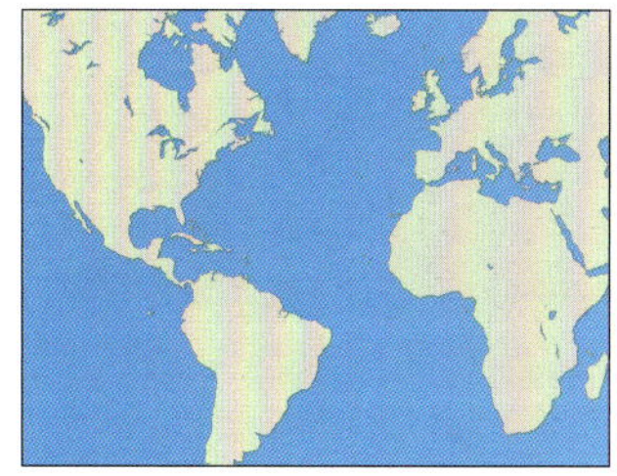

Specimens were found in North America and almost 30 specimens of *Megapnosaurus* were discovered together in fossil beds in Zimbabwe.

HOW BIG IS IT?

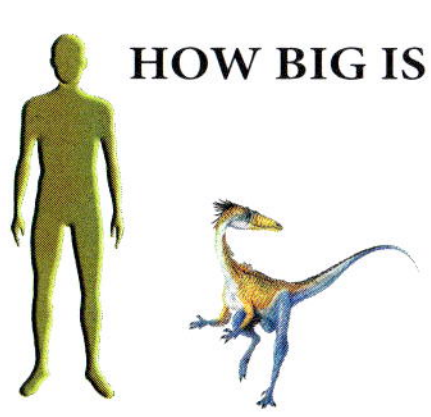

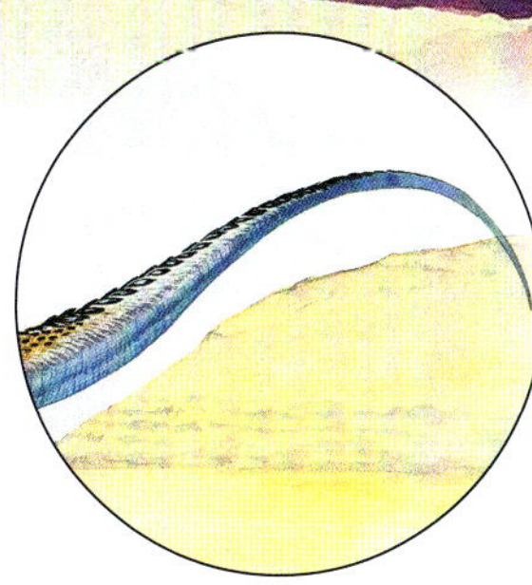

Tail
Held out stiffly behind its body as it ran, the long tail provided *Megapnosaurus* with stability at high speeds.

DINOSAUR

EARLY JURASSIC

TIMELINE (millions of years ago)

540 | **505** | **438** | **408** | **360** | **280** | **248** | **208** | **146** | **65** | **1.8 to today**

Cryolophosaurus

VITAL STATISTICS

Fossil Location	Antarctica
Diet	Carnivorous
Pronunciation	cry-o-LOF-o-sawr-us
Weight	1,160 lb (525 kg)
Length	20 ft (6 m)
Height	(7 ft) 2 m
Meaning of name	"Frozen crested lizard" because it was found on Antartica

FOSSIL EVIDENCE

The fossils found include a partly crushed skull (cranium,) a jawbone (mandible,) 30 vertebrae from the backbone, three hipbones (ilium, iscium, and pubis,) two leg bones (femur and fibula,) plus ankle and foot bones (tibiotarsus and metatarsals). Many of the bones were still in their natural positions and the damage to the skull was possibly caused by a glacier. The fossils had features similar to earlier and later dinosaurs so it was hard to figure out how to classify the finds. At first scientists thought *Cryolophosaurus* was the earliest tetanuran ("stiff tail"). Now scientists think it is more like the later dilophosaurs. It is an important link in theropod evolution.

Where is the toughest place to look for fossils? The answer has to be Antarctica, the frozen region around the South Pole where your eyelashes freeze together. You have to forget about the shovel and pick up the dynamite to do some investigative digging. Yet here, in 1991, paleontologist Dr. William Hammer and his team made a massive discovery—the first carnivorous dinosaur fossil found in Antarctica.

WHERE IN THE WORLD?

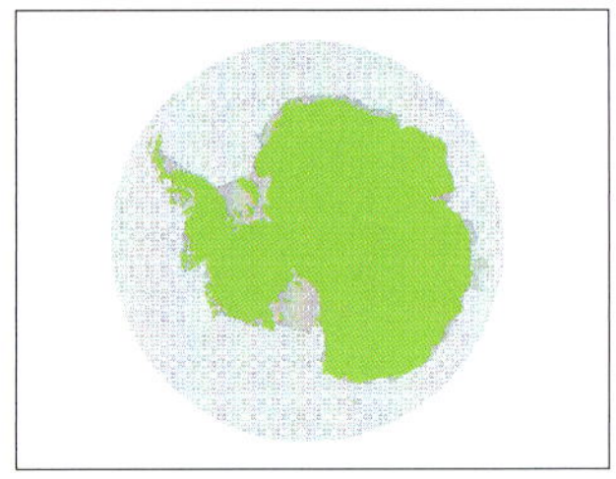

The remains are from Mount Kirkpatrick, located 13,000 ft (4,000 m) up on Antarctica, at 400 miles (640 km) from the South Pole.

Skull
The deep, narrow skull had small horns on either side of the crest. Its sharp, backward-curving serrated teeth provided extra grip.

MEANING OF NAME

When *Cryolophosaurus* lived 195 million years ago, Antarctica was not the frozen land we know today, but a land of Jurassic forests. It was closer to the equator and still attached to Africa. On coastal areas the temperature never dropped below freezing and a wide range of animals survived.

HOW BIG IS IT?

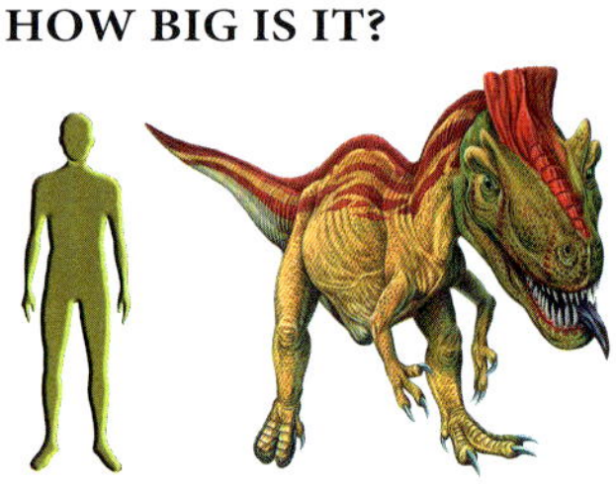

Tail
The tail's weight balanced the dinosaur's body, which was strengthened by interlocking bones.

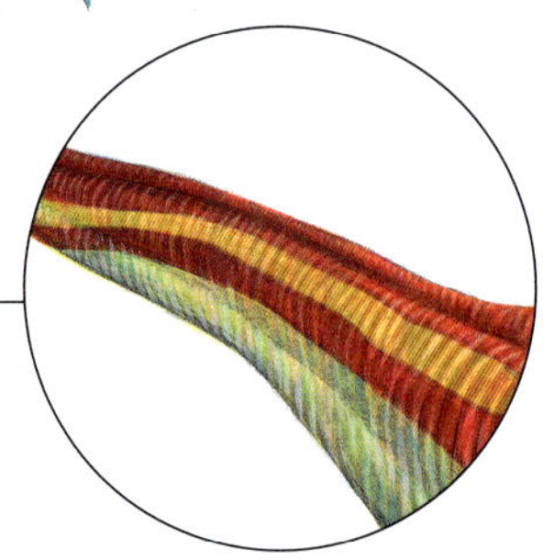

DINOSAUR

EARLY JURASSIC

• **ORDER** • Saurischia • **FAMILY** • Ceratosauria • **GENUS & SPECIES** • *Cryolophosaurus ellioti*

SIZE

At 20 ft (6 m) long and 7 ft (2 m) high, *Cryolophosaurus* was far smaller than later, more advanced carnivores, such as *Allosaurus*, which grew to twice this size.

CREST

The most notable feature of *Cryolophosaurus* is the crest running across its head. Many other dinosaurs have crests, but theirs usually run lengthwise along the skull. This one stands up and fans out over the eyes. It has a comb-like appearance. Because this feature reminded some people of the famous musician Elvis Presley's hairstyle, the dinosaur earned the nickname "Elvisaurus." Like the singer's hair, the crest was for show, probably to attract a mate.

'IMELINE (millions of years ago)

;40	505	438	408	360	280	248	208	146	65	1.8 to today

Dilophosaurus

• **ORDER** • Saurischia • **FAMILY** • Ceratosauria • **GENUS & SPECIES** • *Dilophosaurus wetherel*

VITAL STATISTICS

Fossil Location	United States, China
Diet	Carnivorous
Pronunciation	Die-LOF-oh-SAWR-us
Weight	650-1,000 lb (300-450 kg)
Length	20-23 ft (6-7 m)
Height	5 ft (1.5 m) at the hip
Meaning of name	"Double crested lizard" because of the two thin bone crests atop its head

FOSSIL EVIDENCE

Two men worked for three years cleaning and building the original *Dilophosaurus* skeleton. It was originally named *Megalosaurus* until a more complete fossil was discovered that showed the unique double crests on its head. The crests meant this was a previously undiscovered theropod dinosaur. *Dilophosaurus* had powerful hind limbs and weighed as much as a small horse. It had sharp teeth, but because its jaw was not powerful, these teeth would have been better suited for plucking than stabbing. It probably killed with its hands and feet.

DINOSAUR

EARLY JURASSIC

It had a pretty weak jaw, so *Dilophosaurus* probably relied on its deadly claws to bring down its prey. Three *Dilophosaurus* skeletons were discovered together at one site, suggesting that they traveled around in packs.

Crests
Twin crescent-shaped crests on top of its head may have made *Dilophosaurus* appear attractive to females but scared off possible predators.

HOW BIG IS IT?

Hands
Its flexible hand featured five fingers (two were very small) like its older theropod relatives.

WHERE IN THE WORLD?

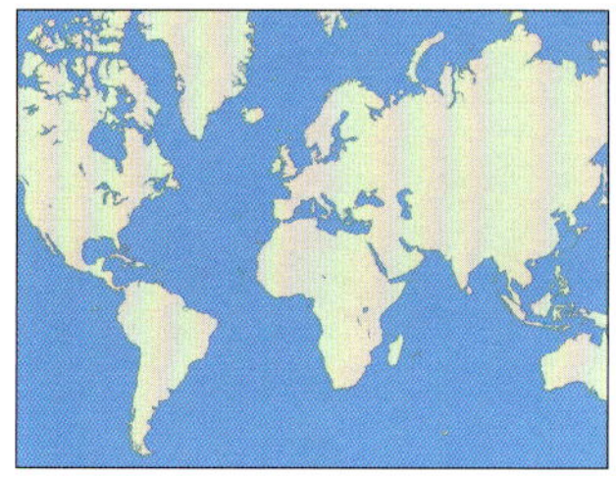

The Early Jurassic beds of northwestern Arizona's Monument Valley are composed of sandstone, siltstone, and shale.

TIMELINE (millions of years ago)

540 | 505 | 438 | 408 | 360 | 280 | 248 | 208 | 146 | 65 | 1.8 to today

Metriacanthosaurus

• **ORDER** • Saurischia • **FAMILY** • Sinraptoridae • **GENUS & SPECIES** • *Metriacanthosaurus parkeri*

VITAL STATISTICS

Fossil Location	England
Diet	Carnivorous
Pronunciation	MET-ri-ah-CAN-thuh-SAWR-us
Weight	1 ton (1.1 tonne)
Length	26 ft (8 m)
Height	6 ft (1.8 m) at the hip
Meaning of Name	"Moderate spined lizard" because its bony spine ridge was less pronounced than in other dinosaurs

When first discussed in 1923, *Metriacanthosaurus* was mistaken as a specimen of *Megalosaurus*. It took forty years to correct the error and recognize *Metriacanthosaurus* as a separate dinosaur.

Spines
Metriacanthosaurus had 10-inch (25 cm) spines along its backbone, which possibly supported a small skin sail, giving the dinosaur a slightly humpbacked appearance.

WHERE IN THE WORLD?

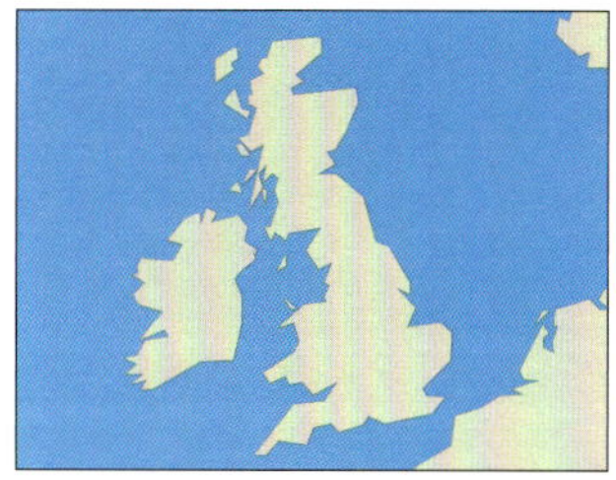

Dorset, England, is a popular place for finding fossils because of the many different species preserved there.

FOSSIL EVIDENCE

Since *Metriacanthosaurus* is known from an incomplete fossil without a skull, paleontologists have argued whether it belongs to the Sinraptoridae or another group within the Tetanurae. We do know that *Metriacanthosaurus* was a large, bipedal carnivore. It had spines along its backbone, but they were not tall enough to hold up a huge sail like those seen on *Dimetrodon* or *Spinosaurus*. Some scientists think that this species is related to the ancestor of spinosaurids.

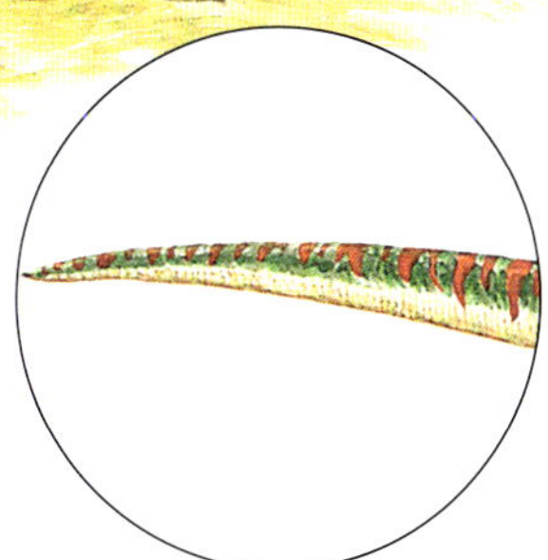

Tail
Its tail was held stiff by a series of bony, interconnecting rods in the vertebrae. The stiff tail helped balance *Metriacanthosaurus*.

HOW BIG IS IT?

DINOSAUR

MID-JURASSIC

TIMELINE (millions of years ago)

540 | 505 | 438 | 408 | 360 | 280 | 248 | 208 | 146 | 65 | 1.8 to today

Ceratosaurus

VITAL STATISTICS

Fossil Location	US, Africa, and Europe
Diet	Carnivorous
Pronunciation	See-RAT-oh-SAWR-us
Weight	1 ton (1.1 tonne)
Length	20 ft (6 m)
Height	7 ft (2 m)
Meaning of name	"Horned lizard" because of its nose horn

FOSSIL EVIDENCE

Classifying *Ceratosaurus* is difficult because it looks like other bipedal predators such as *Allosaurus* and *T. rex*, but these other theropods do not have a line of bony plates down their backs. Other features of *Ceratosaurus* are more avian (bird-like). Teeth provide the only evidence of one species, *C. ingens*, but they suggest a much larger creature that would have been one of the biggest theropods. Teeth marks possibly from *Ceratosaurus* found on prey do not tell us whether it was a predator or scavenger.

DINOSAUR

LATE JURASSIC

Ceratosaurus had large jaws, a horn on its nose and a strip of bony armor down its back. Smaller than _Allosaurus_, who lived at the same time, this meat-eating animal could attack creatures larger than itself.

BACK AND SPINE

In a fight, it always helps to look big and fierce. *Ceratosaurus*'s high back arch and the line of bony plates along its spine helped it look fierce. These features also helped protect it, and may have helped *Ceratosaurus* let off heat to cool down.

HOW BIG IS IT?

ORDER • Saurischia • **FAMILY** • Ceratosauridae • **GENUS & SPECIES** • Several species within the genus *Ceratosaurus*

SNOUT AND EYEBROW HORNS

The feature that gives *Ceratosaurus* its name is the large horn on the snout. Shaped like a blade, its purpose is a mystery. It may have been used in courtship; to attract a mate; or to threaten a rival. It also had a pair of hornlets like ridged eyebrows over the eyes. These horns grew as the animal aged.

WHERE IN THE WORLD?

Fossils have been found in Colorado and Utah, as well as in Portugal and Tanzania.

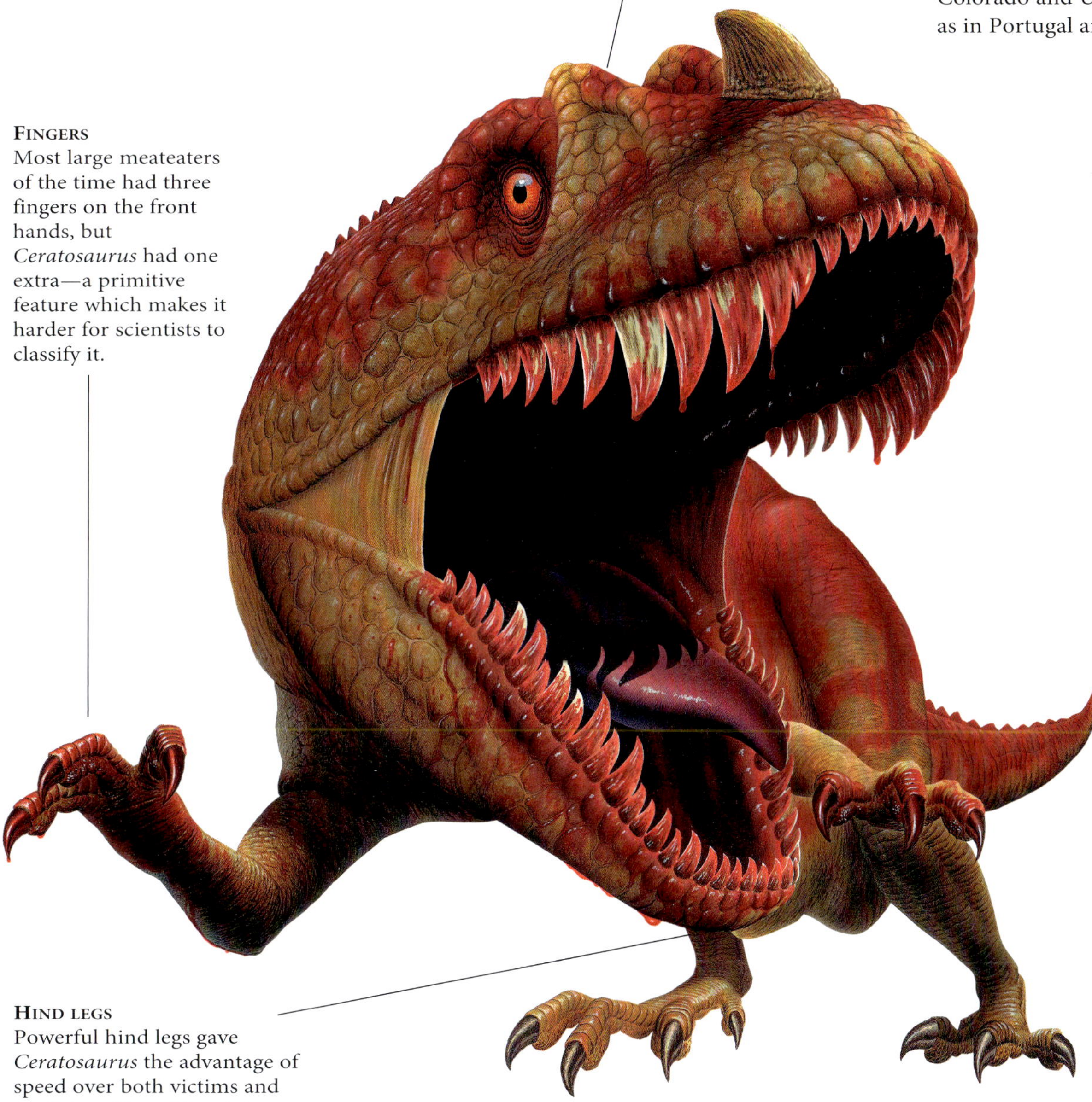

BROW HORNLETS
A pair of hornlets shaped like ridged eyebrows gave some protection to its large eyes in battle.

FINGERS
Most large meateaters of the time had three fingers on the front hands, but *Ceratosaurus* had one extra—a primitive feature which makes it harder for scientists to classify it.

HIND LEGS
Powerful hind legs gave *Ceratosaurus* the advantage of speed over both victims and predators. It could sprint or lunge quickly to surprise and overpower an opponent.

IMELINE (millions of years ago)

40 | 505 | 438 | 408 | 360 | 280 | 248 | 208 | 146 | 65 | 1.8 to today

Ceratosaurus

ORDER • Saurischia • **FAMILY** • Ceratosauridae • **GENUS & SPECIES** • Several species within the genus *Ceratosaurus*

DINOSAUR QUARRIES

The Cleveland-Lloyd Dinosaur Quarry in central Utah is one of two sites in the United States where the fossils of *Ceratosaurus* have been discovered (the other is the Dry Mesa Quarry in Colorado). The Utah quarry, where fossil study began in 1929, has been one of the richest sources of dinosaur fossils in the world. The remains of some 70 creatures from 11 species and more than 12,000 dinosaur bones have been found in the quarry's fossil bed. These have been in the quarry for around 147 million years and were revealed only after erosion wore away the surface mud and covering rock. The bones are mainly separate finds, but when they are put together some may prove to be complete skeletons, like the *Stegosaurus* and *Allosaurus* already built and put on display at the quarry's visitors' center. In 1960, scientists and paleontologists from the University of Utah embarked on a five-year project to dig up further fossils from the quarry. The investigations started up again in 2001, this time to figure out why the quarry is home to so many dinosaur remains.

Chialingosaurus

• **ORDER** • Ornithischia • **FAMILY** • Stegosauridae • **GENUS & SPECIES** • *Chialingosaurus kuar*

VITAL STATISTICS

Fossil Location	China
Diet	Herbivorous
Pronunciation	CHEE-ah-LING-ah-SAWR-us
Weight	331 lb (150 kg)
Length	13 ft (4 m)
Height	Unknown
Meaning of Name	"Chialing lizard" in honor of China's River Chialing

FOSSIL EVIDENCE

Chialingosaurus rambled through the Jurassic landscape on all fours on feet that had hooflike claws. Its hind legs were longer than its front ones, making *Chialingosaurus* look like it sloped forward. Its toothless beak, similar to a modern-day turtle's, snipped off plants. The small cheek teeth chopped up the plant material. Two rows of bony plates ran down its spine from its neck to its midsection. A double row of dangerous spikes ran from the middle of its back down its tail.

DINOSAUR

LATE JURASSIC

***Chialingosaurus*'s brain was approximately the size of a golf ball. The scary spikes sticking out of its back provided this slow dinosaur with some protection against attackers.**

Spikes
Any predator nearing *Chialingosaurus* had to beware of being impaled on the sharp spikes that ran along its back and tail.

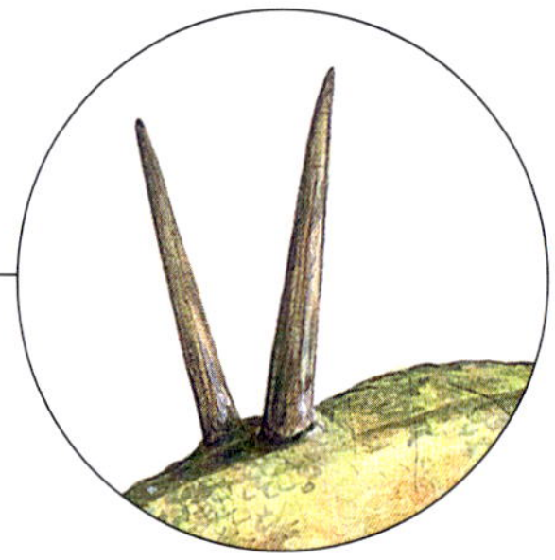

WHERE IN THE WORLD?

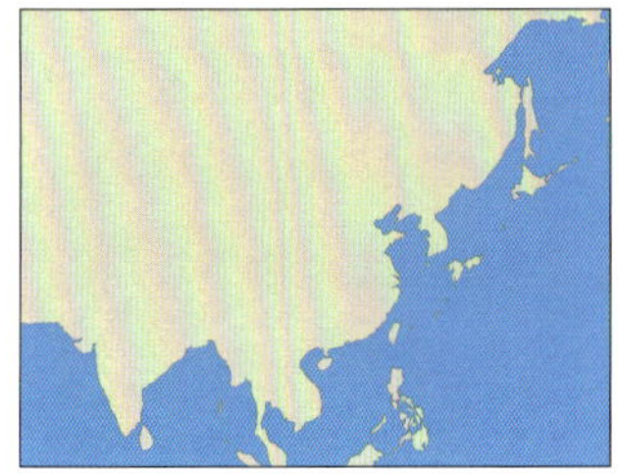

During the Jurassic, when *Chialingosaurus* roamed the Earth, China was part of a supercontinent called Laurasia.

Brain
The size of its tiny brain in comparison to its 331 lb (150 kg) body makes scientists think that *Chialingosaurus* had very low intelligence.

HOW BIG IS IT?

TIMELINE (millions of years ago)

540 | 505 | 438 | 408 | 360 | 280 | 248 | 208 | 146 | 65 | 1.8 to today

Ouranosaurus

• **ORDER** • Ornithischia • **FAMILY** • Unranked • **GENUS & SPECIES** • *Ouranosaurus nigeriensis*

VITAL STATISTICS

Fossil Location	Niger
Diet	Herbivorous
Pronunciation	Ooh-RAN-uh-SAWR-us
Weight	Up to 4 tons (4.4 tonnes)
Length	Up to 23 ft (7 m)
Height	Unknown
Meaning of Name	"Ourane lizard" from the Tuareg tribe of Niger's name for "monitor lizard"

FOSSIL EVIDENCE

Ouranosaurus is known from two complete skeletons found in 1966 in the Echkar Formation in the sands of the Sahara Desert. Originally thought to belong to *Iguanodon*, they were correctly identified ten years later. It is possible that both specimens are male. The skull has a pair of bumps on the nose, but their purpose is unclear, and some scientists think these might be features found only on males. The snout is much longer than *Iguanodon*'s, and seems to have been covered with a horny sheath.

DINOSAUR

EARLY CRETACEOUS

***Ouranosaurus* was a dinosaur with few defenses. Its sail or hump added to its size, which may have been enough to scare off predators. A plant eater, it had a sharp beak well adapted for snipping plants.**

Hump/Sail
Along its back is a feature that may be a sail, for warming and cooling the blood, or a hump for storing food, like on a modern camel.

WHERE IN THE WORLD?

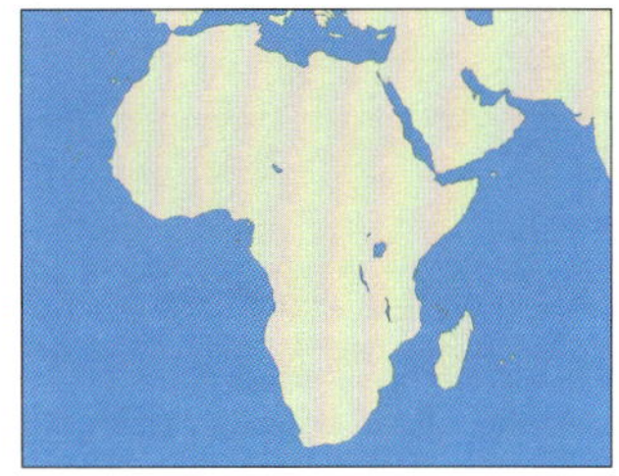

Ouranosaurus was found in Niger, at a time when the region was almost as hot as it is today.

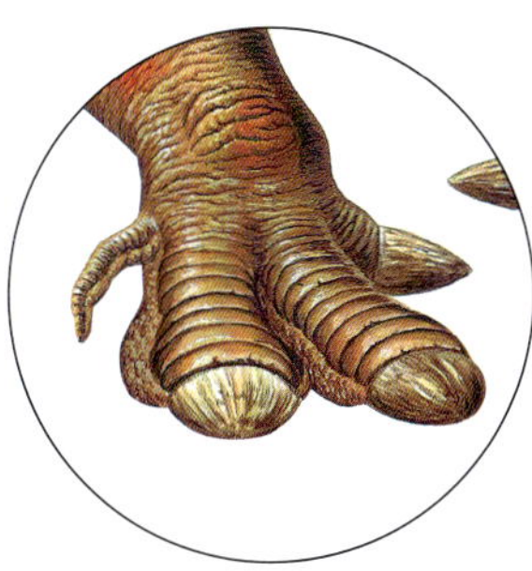

Hands
A thumb claw made a good weapon, while its fifth digit was long and probably used to gather food.

HOW BIG IS IT?

TIMELINE (millions of years ago)

540 | 505 | 438 | 408 | 360 | 280 | 248 | 208 | 146 | 65 | 1.8 to today

Spinosaurus

VITAL STATISTICS

Fossil Location	Egypt, Morocco
Diet	Carnivorous
Pronunciation	Spy-know-SORE-us
Weight	8.85 tons (9,000 kg)
Length	59 ft (18 m)
Height	18 ft 4 in (5.6 m) including "sail"
Meaning of name	"Spine lizard" for the very long vertical (up-and-down) prongs on its vertebrae

The carnivorous dinosaur *Spinosaurus* lived in North Africa about 100 million years ago. It first became known from a description of remains found in the Egyptian desert in 1912 by the German paleontologist Ernst Stromer. These remains were destroyed during World War II, but at least not all of Stromer's work was lost. In 1915, after three years' work, he had recorded a detailed description of his Egyptian finds. The next steps for *Spinosaurus* came 80 years later, when another *Spinosaurus* find was made in Morocco by the Canadian paleontologist Dale Russell.

FOSSIL EVIDENCE

So far, only the skull and backbone of *Spinosaurus* have been described in any great detail. The spines of the dinosaur's backbone were up to 11 times as tall as the vertebrae they grew from. It is thought that these spines were a good deal stronger and larger than the thin rods of pelycosaurs like *Dimetrodon*. In 2005, it was revealed that this skull find was one of the longest known in a carnivorous dinosaur—the skull was estimated to measure 5 ft 9 in (1.75 m) in length with thin snout.

DINOSAUR

MID-CRETACEOUS

HOW BIG IS IT?

SPINOSAURUS SURROUNDINGS

The surroundings in which *Spinosaurus* lived covered most of present-day North Africa before the River Nile system in Egypt had formed. The Egyptian *Spinosaurus* probably lived along a shore that had channels, streams, and tidal flats. It shared mangrove swamps with other large carnivorous predators, such as *Bahariasaurus*, *Carcharodontosaurus* and the 33-foot (10 m)-long prehistoric crocodile, *Stomatosuchus*.

• **ORDER** • Saurischia • **FAMILY** • Spinosauridae • **GENUS & SPECIES** • *Spinosaurus aegyptiacus*

WHERE IN THE WORLD?

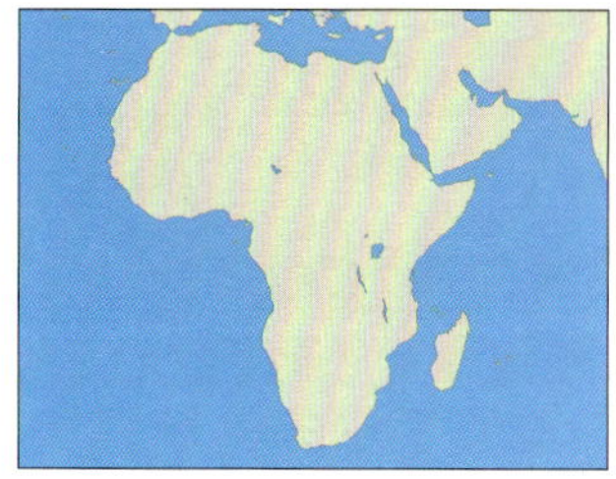

Fossils have been found in the Valley of the Golden Mummies at Bahariya Oasis in the Western Desert of Egypt and in Morocco.

SPINES
Spinosaurus's name comes from the spines that reached from its vertebrae possibly to form a large sail 6 ft (1.8 m) in length from its back.

TEETH
The long, cone-shaped teeth lining *Spinosaurus's* jaws were very unlike most theropod teeth, which were serrated and more flattened. *Spinosaurus's* jaws were perfect for catching and eating the fish on which it lived.

DISCOVERY OF BONES

In 2000, Assistant Professor Josh Smith a professor at Washington University in St. Louis, Missouri, discovered photographs of the *Spinosaurus* bones found by Ernst Stromer in 1912. Until then, it had been thought that after his fossils and other records were destroyed in 1944 the only thing left of Stromer's find were his drawings. The discovery of the photographs made it possible to study Stromer's discoveries more closely than before and to confirm his findings.

MELINE (millions of years ago)

40 | 505 | 438 | 408 | 360 | 280 | 248 | 208 | 146 | 65 | 1.8 to today

Anchiceratops

• **ORDER** • Ornithischia • **FAMILY** • Ceratopsidae • **GENUS & SPECIES** • *Anchiceratops ornat*

VITAL STATISTICS

Fossil Location	Canada
Diet	Herbivorous
Pronunciation	AN-key-SAIR-ah-tops
Weight	5,400 lb (2,470 kg)
Length	15-20 ft (4.5-6 m)
Height	9 ft (2.6 m)
Meaning of name	"Near horn face" because it was originally thought to be closely related to another horned dinosaur, *Centrosaurus*

FOSSIL EVIDENCE

Six skulls have been found, and scientists think that the rest of the body followed the shape of other ceratopsians. All specimens were found near marine sediments, suggesting *Anchiceratops* could have lived in estuaries away from its relatives. The frill is unusual because of its large size, edged by triangular bony points. Such frills may have had defensive or display functions, or may have been used to control body temperature, or to help support a large neck and jaws. The skull supported two large and one small horn.

DINOSAUR

LATE CRETACEOUS

Anchiceratops is one of the rarest chasmosaurines, a group of advanced ceratopsians with three horns, parrotlike beaks and frilled shields. They roamed in herds, digging up plant matter and watching out for _T. rex_, which could pierce their leathery hides.

WHERE IN THE WORLD?

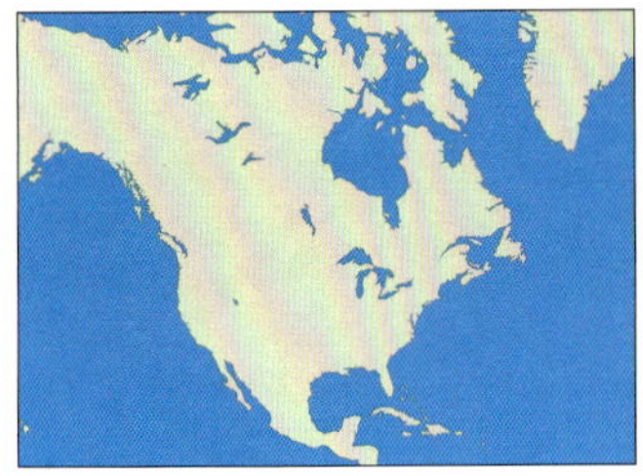

All remains are from the Horseshoe Canyon and Dinosaur Park Formations of Alberta, Canada.

Neck Frill
Its most special feature is the shield-like neck frill topped by six backward-pointing points. Two curved horns stick out from beneath the frill.

HOW BIG IS IT?

Strong Beak
The huge and strong beak was used to cut down low-lying plants, probably mostly conifers, cycads, and ferns but possibly also the newly evolved flowering plants.

TIMELINE (millions of years ago)

540 | 505 | 438 | 408 | 360 | 280 | 248 | 208 | 146 | 65 | 1.8 to today

Arrhinoceratops

• **ORDER** • Ornithischia • **FAMILY** • Ceratopsidae • **GENUS & SPECIES** • *Arrhinoceratops brachyops*

This dinosaur ended up with a misleading name, since its 1925 discoverer decided it had no nose horn. In the 1970s, scientists learned that it did, in fact, have a nose horn. *Arrhinoceratops* is among the last of the long-frilled ceratopsians.

VITAL STATISTICS

Fossil Location	Canada
Diet	Herbivorous
Pronunciation	Ay-RYE-no-SER-uh-tops
Weight	3.9 tons (3.5 tonnes)
Length	20 ft (6 m)
Height	7 ft (2 m)
Meaning of Name	"No nose horn face" based on an incorrect description

FOSSIL EVIDENCE

So far, scientists have only found one fossil which they think belongs to *Arrhinoceratops*. It is a partly crushed skull. Still, scientists use that, along with what they know about the body structure of other ceratopsians, to figure out more about this creature. Its familiar feature is the broad neck frill. It also has two fairly long brow horns and the short, blunt nose horn that was originally missed. The skull is 4 ft 6 in (1.5 m) long and the face is short compared to other dinosaurs of its type.

WHERE IN THE WORLD?

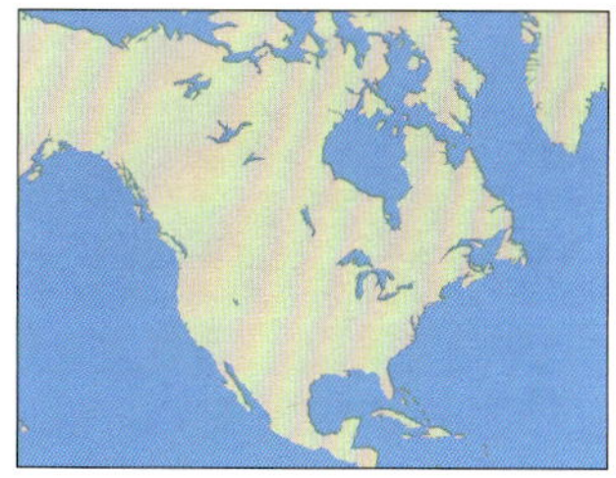

Remains were collected from the Horseshoe Canyon Formation in Alberta, Canada.

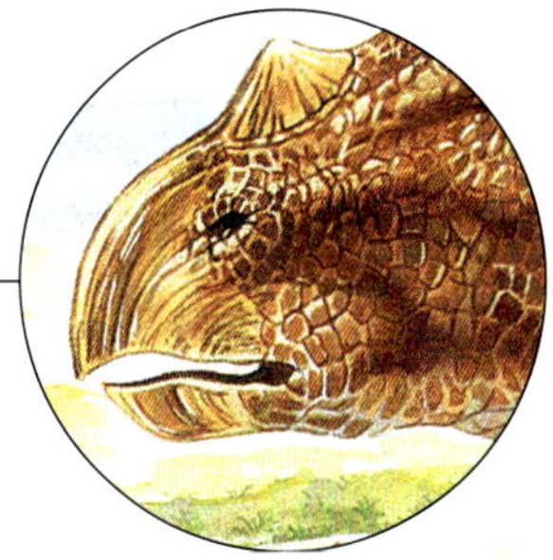

Beak
The toothless beak, common to all ceratopsians, probably had a function related to the herbivorous (plant) diet of the group.

HOW BIG IS IT?

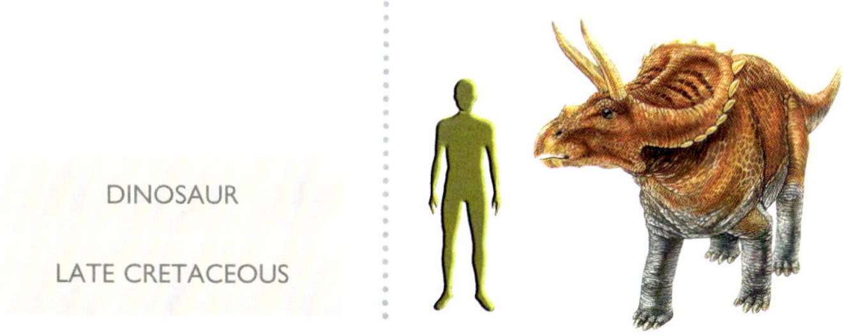

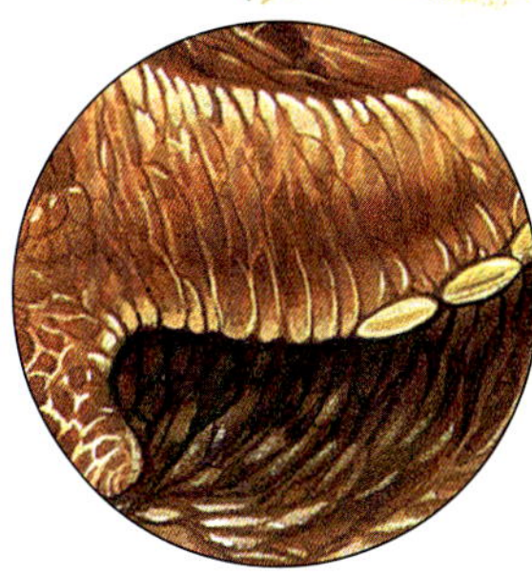

Neck Frill
Two openings in the neck frill made it lighter, and made it easier for *Arrhinoceratops* to lower its head or shake its shield to scare off predators.

TIMELINE (millions of years ago)

540 | 505 | 438 | 408 | 360 | 280 | 248 | 208 | 146 | 65 | 1.8 to today

Bagaceratops

• **ORDER** • Ornithischia • **FAMILY** • Protoceratopsidae • **GENUS & SPECIES** • *Bagaceratops rozhdestvensky*

VITAL STATISTICS

Fossil Location	Mongolia
Diet	Herbivorous
Pronunciation	BAG-uh-CER-uh-TOPS
Weight	50 lb (22 kg)
Length	3 ft (1 m)
Height	20 in (50 cm)
Meaning of Name	"Small horned face" as it is smaller than its relatives

FOSSIL EVIDENCE

There are five complete and 17 broken skulls of *Bagaceratops*, young and old, which help paleontologists to build a clear picture of its appearance and how it developed. It was about the size of a pig and had a small triangular frill forming a shield around its neck. This was a desert dweller, possibly roaming in herds and digging up low-level plants and roots with its toothless sharp beak—it probably could not stand on its hind legs. Its close relatives had no horns, but *Bagaceratops* had a small bony bump on its snout.

DINOSAUR

LATE CRETACEOUS

Bagaceratops appears to be a smaller, less advanced version of _Protoceratops_, but it isn't. _Bagaceratops_ actually walked the planet after, rather than before, _Protoceratops_.

Teeth
There were ten grinding teeth on each side of the jaw, each with a replacement growing underneath, so broken teeth were not a problem.

WHERE IN THE WORLD?

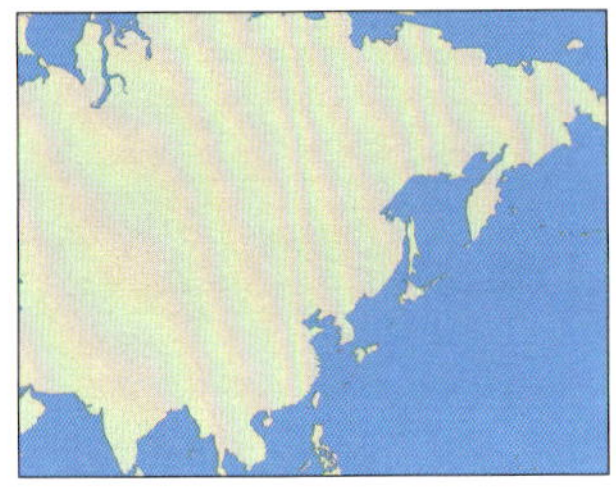

All the remains have been found preserved in desert sandstone in Mongolia.

HOW BIG IS IT?

Bony Knob
The bony knob on the face turned into well-developed horns on ceratopsians, such as *Centrosaurus* and *Triceratops*.

TIMELINE (millions of years ago)

540 | 505 | 438 | 408 | 360 | 280 | 248 | 208 | 146 | 65 | 1.8 to today

Brachylophosaurus

• **ORDER** • Ornithischia
• **FAMILY** • Hadrosauridae • **GENUS & SPECIES** • *Brachylophosaurus canadensis*

VITAL STATISTICS

Fossil Location	North America
Diet	Herbivorous
Pronunciation	BRACK-ee-LOAF-ah-SAW-rus
Weight	2,900-5,950 lb (1,300-2,700 kg)
Length	23 ft (7 m)
Height	9 ft (2.8 m)
Meaning of Name	"Short crested lizard" after its crest feature

FOSSIL EVIDENCE

Brachylophosaurus was already known as a crested hadrosaur when the mummified remains were discovered in 2000. About 80 percent of the skin and muscles were intact, as well as the half-digested remains of 40 different types of plants and some evergreen wood in its gut. The young dinosaur probably got trapped on a sandbar and was naturally mummified by the hot air and covered in sand. Studies of other remains of this crested dinosaur have shown that it often got tumors.

DINOSAUR

LATE CRETACEOUS

In 2000 one of the most extraordinary dinosaur finds was made when a mummified young *Brachylophosaurus* was found in the Montana sandstone. The find included the skin, muscles, and even the last meal the animal ate.

WHERE IN THE WORLD?

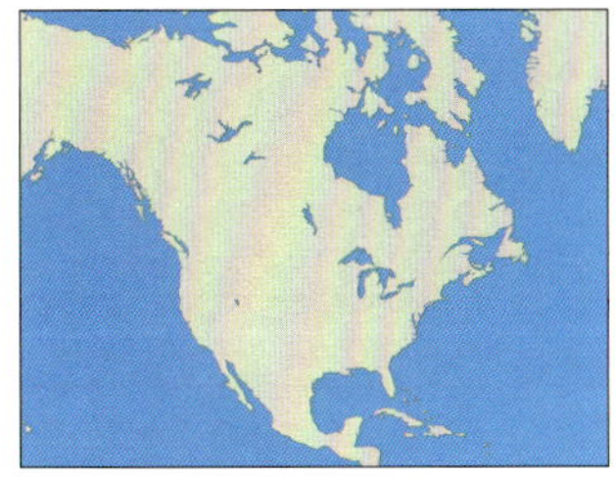

Fossils and other remains are from Montana's Judith River Formation and the Oldman Formation of Alberta, Canada.

Crest
This animal had a broad, flat crest with a spike above its eyes. This spike, being solid, was possibly used for head-butting contests.

Beak
The beak of the upper jaw was wider than other hadrosaurs'. *Brachylophosaurus* also had longer forelimbs.

HOW BIG IS IT?

TIMELINE (millions of years ago)

Chasmosaurus

• **ORDER** • Ornithischia • **FAMILY** • Ceratopsidae • **GENUS & SPECIES** • Several species within the genus *Chasmosaurus*

VITAL STATISTICS

Fossil Location	Canada, US
Diet	Herbivorous
Pronunciation	KAS-mo-SAWR-us
Weight	4 tons (3.6 tonnes)
Length	16-20 ft (5-6 m)
Height	10 ft (3 m)
Meaning of Name	"Chasm lizard" because of the holes in its frill

FOSSIL EVIDENCE

Chasmosaurus was a common ceratopsian that roamed in herds. Its special feature was a huge neck frill about 5 ft (1.4 m) long and 3 ft (1 m) wide. Although it looked dangerous, the frill probably was not much of a weapon. It may have been more important for display and possibly helping to control body temperature. *Chasmosaurus* had three facial horns, two large brow horns and one shorter, wider horn on the nose.

DINOSAUR

LATE CRETACEOUS

What was *Chasmosaurus's* big triangular frill for? It would have looked fierce, especially if the animals lined up facing their attackers, but it was too delicate to offer any real protection.

Fossilized Skin
Fossilized skin remains show that *Chasmosaurus* had evenly spaced, five- or six-sided bony knobs, each with a diameter of 2 in (5 cm).

WHERE IN THE WORLD?

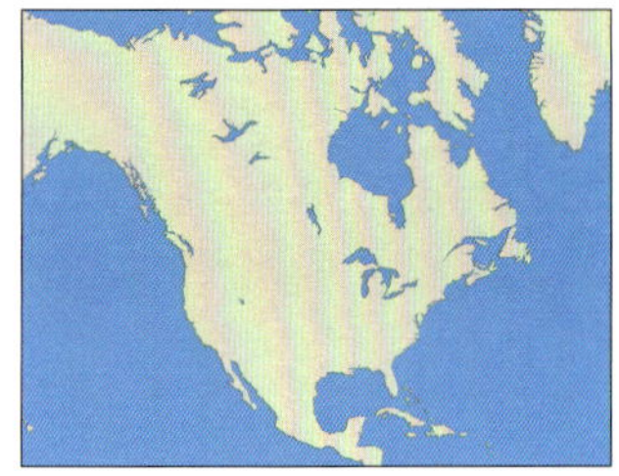

Over a long area of land from Alberta, Canada, to Texas.

Brow Horns
Some specimens have long brow horns, while others have short ones. It is possible that longer horns appeared on the males.

HOW BIG IS IT?

TIMELINE (millions of years ago)

540 | 505 | 438 | 408 | 360 | 280 | 248 | 208 | 146 | 65 | 1.8 to today

Chirostenotes

• **ORDER** • Saurischia • **FAMILY** • Caenagnathidae • **GENUS & SPECIES** • *Chirostenotes pergracilis, C. elegans*

VITAL STATISTICS

Fossil Location	Canada
Diet	Possibly omnivorous
Pronunciation	KIE-roh-STEN-oh-teez
Weight	66 lb (30 kg)
Length	7 ft (2 m)
Height	28 in (70 cm)
Meaning of Name	"Narrow hand" after its unusual hands, the first part found

FOSSIL EVIDENCE

Although the hands, feet, and jaws had been discovered (in 1924, 1932, and 1936,) it took the reconstruction of the "lost" skeleton in 1988 to help scientists figure out the remains were from the same beast. *Chirostenotes* was a lightly built birdlike theropod with three thin, clawed fingers on each hand, the middle one being bigger than the others. *Chirostenotes* would have been a quick, athletic predator. Mostly a carnivore, it may have been omnivorous. Various species have been found; some were even larger and heavier than the measurements given here.

DINOSAUR

LATE CRETACEOUS

***Chirostenotes* is the skeleton in the dinosaur family cupboard—literally! Only partial remains were known until a specimen that had been gathering dust for 60 years was rediscovered in 1988 and identified.**

WHERE IN THE WORLD?

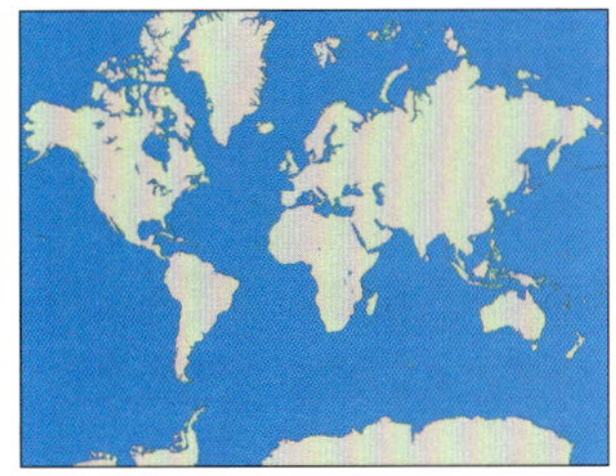

Remains have been found in the Dinosaur Park Formation in Alberta, Canada.

Crest
The head was topped with a crest similar to that of the *Oviraptor*, which lived two million years later, suggesting that the two dinosaurs are related.

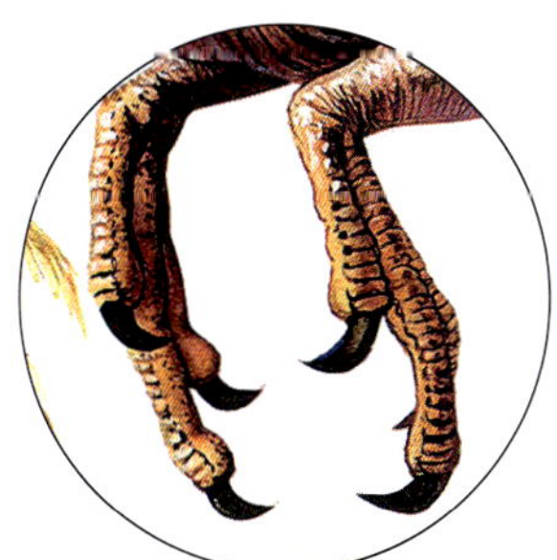

Hands
The three-fingered hands seem particularly well suited to grabbing fish, snatching eggs, and prying insects out of bark.

HOW BIG IS IT?

TIMELINE (millions of years ago)

540 | 505 | 438 | 408 | 360 | 280 | 248 | 208 | 146 | 65 | 1.8 to today

Corythosaurus

• **ORDER** • Ornithischia • **FAMILY** • Hadrosauridae • **GENUS & SPECIES** • *Corythosaurus casuariu*

VITAL STATISTICS

Fossil Location	Canada, Western US
Diet	Herbivorous
Pronunciation	Co-RITH-oh-SAWR-us
Weight	5.5 tons (5 tonnes)
Length	30 ft (9 m)
Height	6.5 ft (2 m) at the hips
Meaning of Name	"Helmet lizard" because its crest is like those worn by Corinthian soldiers

FOSSIL EVIDENCE

Around 20 skulls have been found, often in the same location, which suggests that *Corythosaurus* traveled in groups. The elaborate crest was not only decorative—it was hollow and contains nasal passages that may have allowed it to make loud, low-pitched calls. The crest may also have helped with cooling, sense of smell, and even played a role in its courtship rituals. Some skin remains have survived through natural mummification. These reveal a rough surface of tiny bumps with larger scales on the belly.

DINOSAUR

LATE CRETACEOUS

This was one of the most abundant duck-billed dinosaurs of western North America, best known for its splendid crest that not only looked impressive but may have helped it make trumpeting calls.

WHERE IN THE WORLD?

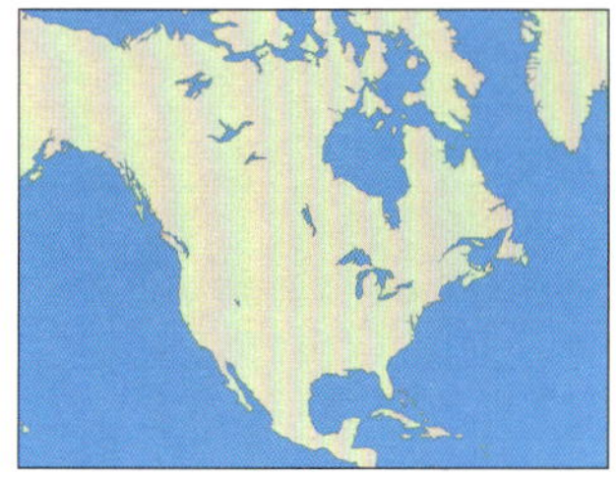

Numerous remains have been found in Alberta, Canada, and Montana.

Eyes
Large eyes on either side of the head allowed it to see in two different directions at once, helping it avoid predators.

HOW BIG IS IT?

Hind Legs
Corythosaurus could stand on its hind legs and stretch its neck to pull food from high branches with its toothless beak. The food was then ground up by hundreds of cheek teeth.

TIMELINE (millions of years ago)

540 | 505 | 438 | 408 | 360 | 280 | 248 | 208 | 146 | 65 | 1.8 to today

Diceratus

• **ORDER** • Ornithischia • **FAMILY** • Ceratopsidae • **GENUS & SPECIES** • *Diceratus hatcheri*

VITAL STATISTICS

Fossil Location	United States
Diet	Herbivorous
Pronunciation	Die-SAIR-ah-tus
Weight	12.1 tons (11 tonnes)
Length	Up to 30 ft (9 m)
Height	9 ft (2.7 m)
Meaning of Name	"Two-horned" after the horns on its face

FOSSIL EVIDENCE

All descriptions of this creature are based on one poorly preserved skull which was discovered in 1905. This horned dinosaur was thought to be a very large type of *Triceratops* for decades, but there are big differences between them. It has a rounded stump where the nose horn should be, and the brow horns are almost vertical, while the neck frills are shaped differently. By the time this was understood, the original name of *Diceratops* had been given to a group of insects. The dinosaur was renamed *Diceratus* in 2008.

DINOSAUR

LATE CRETACEOUS

You could forgive *Diceratus* for having an identity crisis. It was thought to be a type of *Triceratops* for years. Then scientists decided it was really a genus (or group) of its own.

Frill
Skin-covered holes in the frill made this feature lighter and provided anchors for the large muscles needed to power the jaw.

HOW BIG IS IT?

Legs
Diceratus would have moved slowly on four strong legs, probably reaching only 1-2.5 mph (2-4 km/h) as it browsed low-lying plants.

WHERE IN THE WORLD?

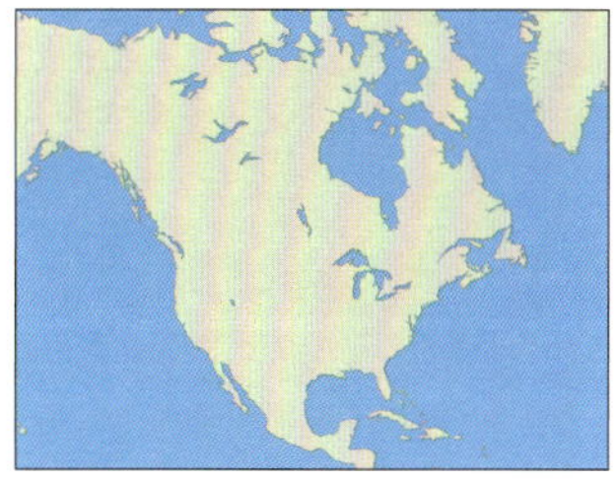

The only specimen was found in Wyoming.

IMELINE (millions of years ago)

40	505	438	408	360	280	248	208	146	65	1.8 to today

Einiosaurus

• **ORDER** • Ornithischia • **FAMILY** • Ceratopsidae • **GENUS & SPECIES** • *Einiosaurus procurvicornis*

VITAL STATISTICS

Fossil Location	United States
Diet	Herbivorous
Pronunciation	Eye-nee-o-SAWR-us
Weight	1.8-2 tons (2-2.2. tonnes)
Length	16-20 ft (5-6 m)
Height	Unknown
Meaning of name	"Bison lizard" named to honor the Black Feet Tribe, on whose land the fossils were found and refer to the idea that ceratopsians were the "buffalo" of the Cretaceous

FOSSIL EVIDENCE

Einiosaurus was discovered in 1985, starting an excavation that was not completed until 1989. Its completed description came in 1995. The discovery was made in the Two Medicine Formation, Montana, a deposit with lots of dinosaur specimens, including one of the most important finds in the world. The evidence suggests that *Einiosaurus* lived in a semiarid climate, with a long dry season. From three skulls found, some think the special nose horn was a feature found only on adult males.

DINOSAUR

LATE CRETACEOUS

Einiosaurus's forward-curving nose horn (which some think looks like a can opener) sets it apart from other horned dinosaurs. It looked intimidating, but _Einiosaurus's_ best defense was that it probably lived in herds.

WHERE IN THE WORLD?

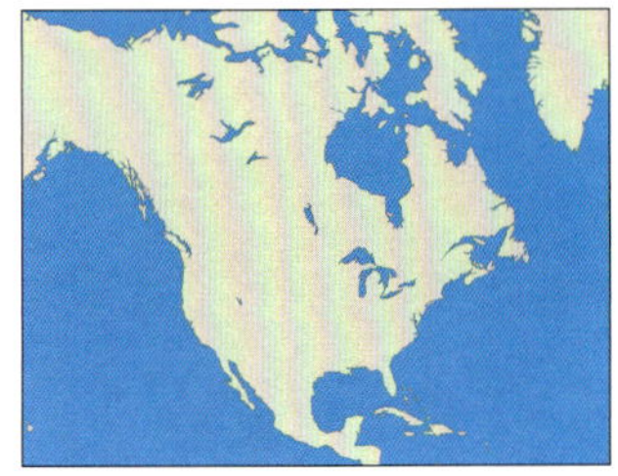

To date, *Einiosaurus* has been located only in Montana.

Spikes
Two spikes at the top of its bony frill scared predators, though they probably offered little help as weapons.

Legs
It is not clear whether *Einiosaurus* stood upright, like an elephant, or had a more spread-out posture, like a lizard.

HOW BIG IS IT?

TIMELINE (millions of years ago)

540 | 505 | 438 | 408 | 360 | 280 | 248 | 208 | 146 | 65 | 1.8 to today

Hypacrosaurus

• **ORDER** • Ornithischia • **FAMILY** • Hadrosauridae • **GENUS & SPECIES** • *Hypacrosaurus altispinus*

VITAL STATISTICS

Fossil Location	Canada, United States
Diet	Herbivorous
Pronunciation	Hi-PACK-roe-SAWR-us
Weight	1.3 tons (1.4 tonnes)
Length	30 ft (9 m)
Height	Unknown
Meaning of Name	"Almost the top lizard" because it was almost as large as *Tyrannosaurus rex*

FOSSIL EVIDENCE

The first specimen of *Hypacrosaurus* was found near Alberta, Canada, in 1912. Then, in the 1990s, a find in Devil's Coulee, in southwestern Alberta, provided much information about young *Hypacrosaurus*. A nest was found, and inside, lined up in rows, were eight eggs, each the size of a cantaloupe. It is possible that the nest was originally covered over with sand or plant matter. Hatchlings were found nearby. This makes scientists think *Hypacrosaurus* created nesting sites, in which multiple nests could be guarded.

DINOSAUR

LATE CRETACEOUS

Hypacrosaurus **foraged (searched) for food on all four legs but walked and ran on two legs.**

Crest
A hollow crest may have acted as an echo chamber, which would have helped *Hypacrosaurus* to make sounds. Or, it may have sharpened its sense of smell.

WHERE IN THE WORLD?

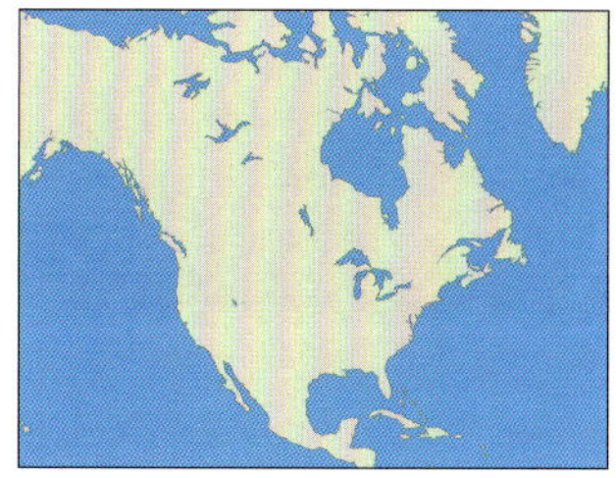

Hypacrosaurus was found in western North America, in what is now Alberta, Canada, and Montana.

Mouth
Forty rows of tightly packed cheek teeth helped it to grind up its food, which may have included pine needles, fruit, twigs, and possibly even flowering plants.

HOW BIG IS IT?

IMELINE (millions of years ago)

40 | 505 | 438 | 408 | 360 | 280 | 248 | 208 | 146 | 65 | 1.8 to today

Jaxartosaurus

• **ORDER** • Ornithischia • **FAMILY** • Hadrosauridae • **GENUS & SPECIES** • *Jaxartosaurus aralens*

VITAL STATISTICS

Fossil Location	Kazakhstan, China
Diet	Herbivorous
Pronunciation	Jax-SAHR-toh-SAWR-us
Weight	Unknown
Length	26-30 ft (8-9 m)
Height	Unknown
Meaning of name	"Jaxartes lizard" after Jaxartes, the ancient name for the Syr Darya River near where the fossil was found in Kazakhstan

FOSSIL EVIDENCE

Little is known about *Jaxartosaurus*. It is known only from fossil pieces, including the skull roof and braincase. Like other duck-billed dinosaurs, it had a series of hinges and joints in its skull, which may have helped to protect its brain—and also its teeth—stopping them from breaking under impact. One joint is like a joint found on a modern crocodile, which acts as a shock absorber when the jaws snap shut. Fossilized teeth show lots of wear, which is a sign of constant chewing.

DINOSAUR

LATE CRETACEOUS

***Jaxartosaurus* was an herbivore that chopped plants with its toothless beak, chewing them with large flat-topped cheek teeth. Adults had crests, though the female's was probably smaller.**

Crest
Air passages in its helmet-like crest linked its throat and nostrils, possibly helping *Jaxartosaurus* to make a trumpeting noise.

WHERE IN THE WORLD?

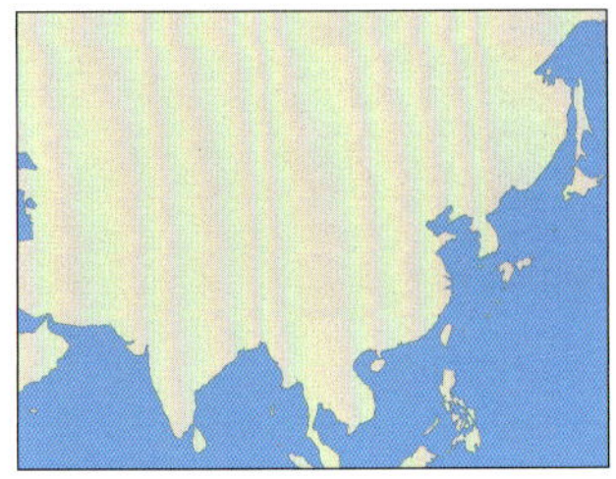

Jaxartosaurus was located in Asia, specifically China and Kazakhstan.

HOW BIG IS IT?

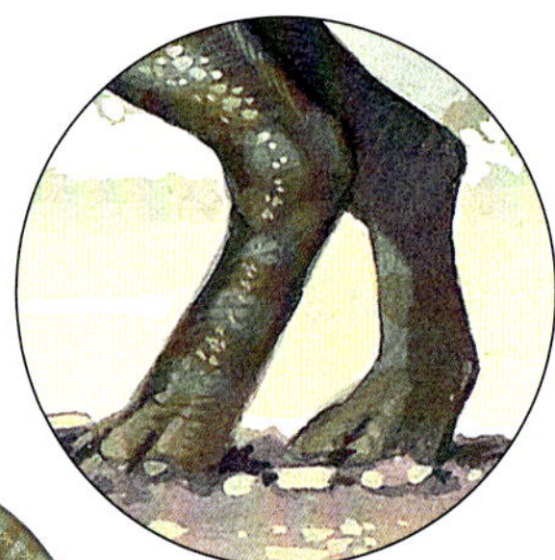

Legs
Jaxartosaurus possibly fed on all fours, but perhaps when it sensed danger it got up on its hind legs to run, stiffening its tail for balance.

TIMELINE (millions of years ago)

540 | 505 | 438 | 408 | 360 | 280 | 248 | 208 | 146 | 65 | 1.8 to today

Microceratus

• **ORDER** • Ornithischia • **FAMILY** • Protoceratopsidae • **GENUS & SPECIES** • *Microceratus gobiensis*

VITAL STATISTICS

Fossil Location	Southern Mongolia, northern China
Diet	Herbivorous
Pronunciation	MY-cro-SAIR-ah-tus
Weight	9-15 lb (4-7 kg)
Length	32 in (80 cm)
Height	Unknown
Meaning of Name	"Tiny horned face"

FOSSIL EVIDENCE

The fossil evidence for small dinosaurs is generally very rare but often better preserved and more complete than the fossils of much larger creatures. They are less common because they are more delicate but they are more likely to be complete because larger carcasses (remains of a dead animal) often get scattered and weather more before burial. *Microceratus* was no longer than 32 in (80 cm); its relative *Protoceratops* was 6 ft (1.8 m). It was first described in 1953 as *Microceratops*, but its name had already been assigned to an ichneumon wasp. A new name—*Microceratus*—was therefore created for it in 2008.

DINOSAUR

LATE CRETACEOUS

Microceratus is the smallest-known horned dinosaur. It had a frill and a horny beak and was a very fast runner so it could easily escape an attacker.

Beak
With its parrotlike beak, *Microceratus* probably fed on the most common plants of its time, including conifers, ferns, and cycads, cropping the leaves and needles.

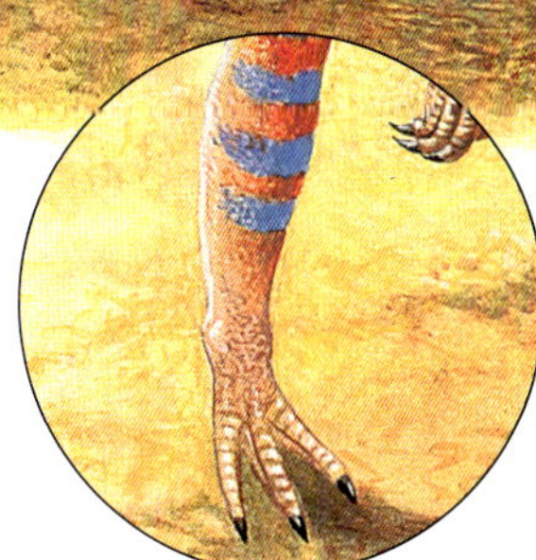

Hind Legs *Microceratus* was bipedal and had shins twice as long as its thighs—as well as long narrow feet—that made it a fast runner.

HOW BIG IS IT?

WHERE IN THE WORLD?

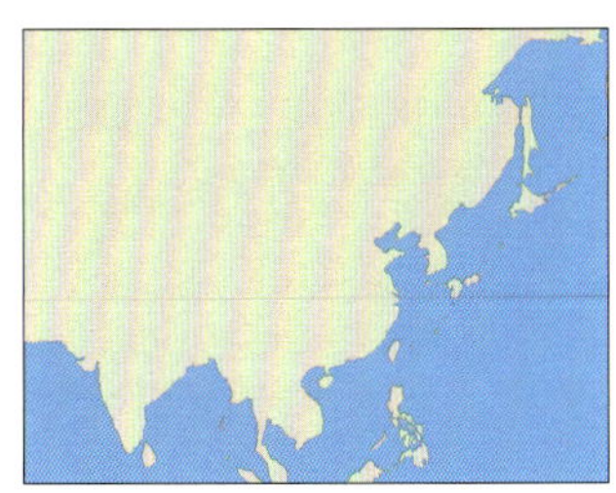

Microceratus was found in what is now China and Mongolia.

TIMELINE (millions of years ago)

540	505	438	408	360	280	248	208	146	65	1.8 to today

Montanoceratops

• **ORDER** • Ornithischia • **FAMILY** • Leptoceratopsida
• **GENUS & SPECIES** • *Montanoceratops cerorhynchc*

VITAL STATISTICS

Fossil Location	United States, Canada
Diet	Herbivorous
Pronunciation	Mon-TAN-oh-SAIR-ah-tops
Weight	992 lb (450 kg)
Length	6-10 ft (1.8-3 m)
Height	Unknown
Meaning of Name	"Montana horned face" after the state of Montana where the fossil was found

FOSSIL EVIDENCE

The first specimens found for *Montanoceratops* were just pieces: a partial skull (most of which was missing,) some vertebrae, and pieces of pelvis and hind legs. At first scientists thought they belonged to *Leptoceratops*. Later discoveries changed the scientists' minds. The finds also showed that *Montanoceratops* might have been a herding animal that protected its young. Bonebeds containing many specimens in the same area are signs of herding behavior.

DINOSAUR

LATE CRETACEOUS

***Montanoceratops* was a medium-sized horned dinosaur. It had a small frill and nose horn, a powerful jaw, and a parrotlike beak.**

Hind Legs
Its hind legs were longer than its front legs, making *Montanoceratops*'s back slope slightly forward.

WHERE IN THE WORLD?

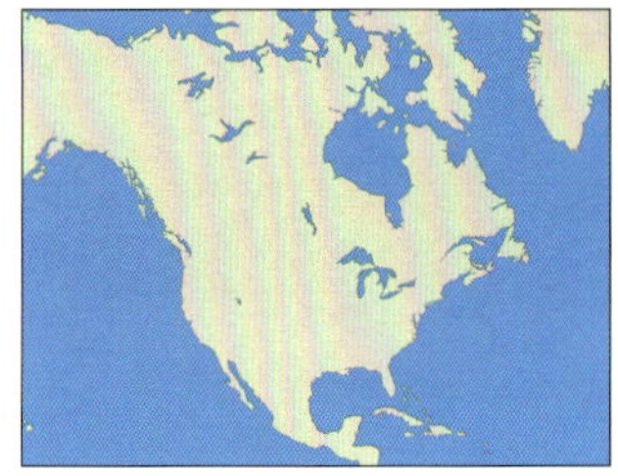

Montanoceratops was found in Montana and Alberta, Canada.

HOW BIG IS IT?

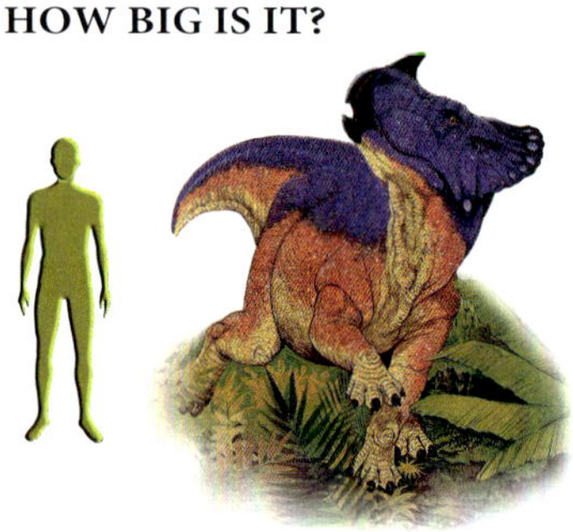

Frills
The frill of what is thought by some to be the male *Montanoceratops* was larger than that of the female, which is a sign that it might have been used for attracting a mate.

TIMELINE (millions of years ago)

540 | 505 | 438 | 408 | 360 | 280 | 248 | 208 | 146 | 65 | 1.8 to today

Nipponosaurus

• **ORDER** • Ornithischia • **FAMILY** • Hadrosauridae • **GENUS & SPECIES** • *Nipponosaurus sachalinensis*

VITAL STATISTICS

Fossil Location	Japan
Diet	Herbivorous
Pronunciation	Ni-PON-oh-SAWR-us
Weight	Unknown
Length	25 ft (7.6 m)
Height	Unknown
Meaning of name	"Japanese lizard" because its fossil was found on an island that was owned by Japan at the time

The first dinosaur to be found on Japanese soil, *Nipponosaurus* was a small duck-billed dinosaur. Walking on two legs, it had a broad head, short neck, and a long beak.

Crest
A low, dome-shaped crest, which was connected to its nose and throat by air passages, possibly helped it to make sound.

WHERE IN THE WORLD?

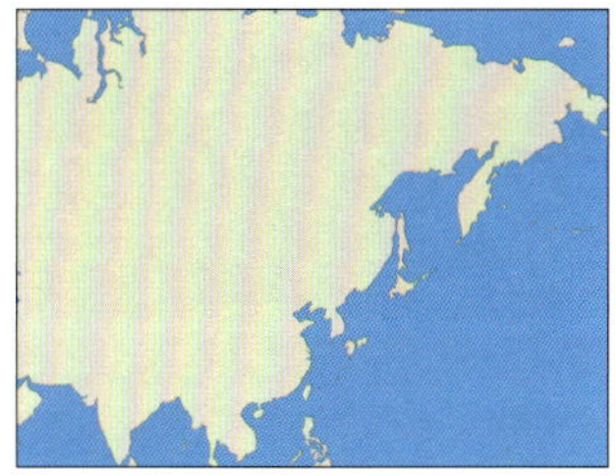

Nipponosaurus was found in the south of Sakhalin Island, a region that is now part of Russia.

FOSSIL EVIDENCE

Nipponosaurus was discovered in 1934, during the construction of a hospital, and more material from the same specimen was recovered in 1937. It has been identified from a poorly preserved, incomplete skeleton, including fragments of the skull, teeth, parts of the forelimbs, and most of the hind limbs. The specimen is thought to be about 60 percent complete. Still, little is known about *Nipponosaurus*. Some paleontologists argue that the specimen is, in fact, a young *Jaxartosaurus*, another hadrosaur.

Mouth
Its beak was toothless but it had hundreds of small teeth, for grinding the plant material it ate.

HOW BIG IS IT?

DINOSAUR

LATE CRETACEOUS

TIMELINE (millions of years ago)

540	505	438	408	360	280	248	208	146	65	1.8 to today

Pachyrhinosaurus

• **ORDER** • Ornithischia • **FAMILY** • Ceratopsidae • **GENUS & SPECIES** • *Pachyrhinosaurus canadensis*

VITAL STATISTICS

Fossil Location	Canada
Diet	Herbivorous
Pronunciation	Pack-ee-RINE-oh-SAWR-us
Weight	1.8 tons (2 tonnes)
Length	7 ft (2 m)
Height	Unknown
Meaning of Name	"Thick-nosed lizard," after the lump of bone on its nose

When threatened, *Pachyrhinosaurus* may have charged its attacker, just like the modern rhinoceros does. Its large skull was built to butt and shove so it could put up a strong defense against enemies.

WHERE IN THE WORLD?

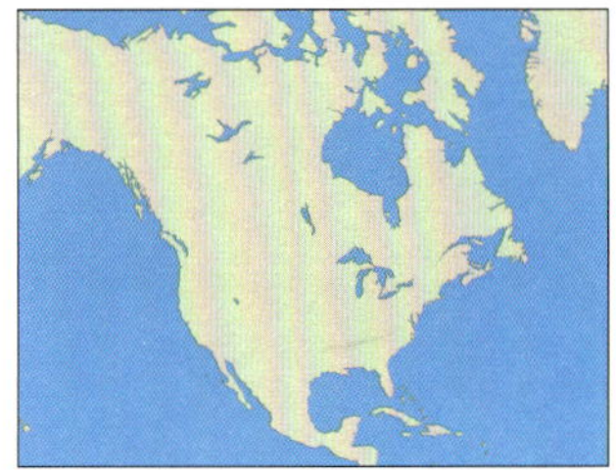

Pachyrhinosaurus was found in Alberta, Canada.

Nose
Pachyrhinosaurus had a large bony pad on its nose. Some paleontologists think this was the base of a nose horn, even though no fossil showing this horn has been found.

FOSSIL EVIDENCE

It is from the fossil evidence that we know *Pachyrhinosaurus* probably traveled in herds. In 1972, a huge group was found at Pipestone Creek, Alberta, in a bonebed from which 14 skulls and 3,500 bones were removed. The specimens included young and old, a sign that *Pachyrhinosaurus* cared for its young. The animals were probably trying to cross a river, or were overcome by a flash flood.

Frill
Horns grew from the edge of its neck frill, and one small spike stuck up from the center.

HOW BIG IS IT?

DINOSAUR

LATE CRETACEOUS

TIMELINE (millions of years ago)

540	505	438	408	360	280	248	208	146	65	1.8 to today

Pentaceratops

• ORDER • Ornithischia **• FAMILY •** Ceratopsidae **• GENUS & SPECIES •** *Pentaceratops sternbergii*

VITAL STATISTICS

FOSSIL LOCATION	Southwestern US
DIET	Herbivorous
PRONUNCIATION	PEN-ta-SAIR-ah-tops
WEIGHT	6 tons (6.6 tonnes)
LENGTH	25 ft (7.5 m)
HEIGHT	Unknown
MEANING OF NAME	"Five-horned face" in reference to its three face horns and two cheek spikes

FOSSIL EVIDENCE

Pentaceratops is known from nine skulls and several skeletons. As an herbivore, it probably fed on the most common plants of its time: conifers, cycads, and ferns. Fossil records show scientists that there were fewer species of plants and animals toward the end of the Cretaceous period. Scientists think there might have been a major environmental event some time after the *Pentaceratops* died out, which seems to have blocked sunlight. It might have been a meteor. Without sunlight, plants could not survive. The herbivores who needed those plants for food died out, too.

DINOSAUR

LATE CRETACEOUS

***Pentaceratops* had one of the largest skulls of any land-based vertebrate, and its frill and horns helped scare both predators and rivals. Unlike many dinosaurs, this herbivore could chew well with its cheek teeth.**

SPIKES
Pentaceratops took its name from the large horns on its brow, a short nose horn, and two spikes sticking up from under its eyes.

FRILL
Pentaceratops's frill reached halfway down its back and was edged with bony knobs. It was not too heavy, though, because large fenestrae, or holes, cut down its weight.

HOW BIG IS IT?

WHERE IN THE WORLD?

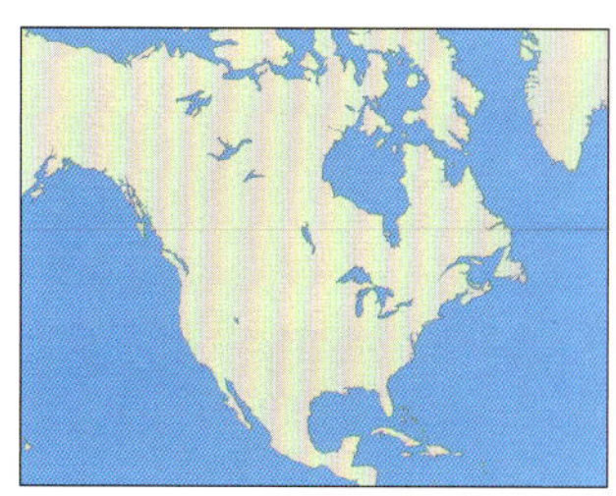

Pentaceratops was located in what is now New Mexico.

MELINE (millions of years ago)

0 | 505 | 438 | 408 | 360 | 280 | 248 | 208 | 146 | 65 | 1.8 to today

Prosaurolophus

• **ORDER** • Ornithischia • **FAMILY** • Hadrosauridae • **GENUS & SPECIES** • *Prosaurolophus maximu*

VITAL STATISTICS

Fossil Location	Canada, United States
Diet	Herbivorous
Pronunciation	PROH-saw-ROL-off-us
Weight	1.8 tons (2 tonnes)
Length	26 ft (8 m)
Height	Unknown
Meaning of Name	"Before *Saurolophus*" because at first it was thought to be an early relative of *Saurolophus*

FOSSIL EVIDENCE

Prosaurolophus was described in 1916 by Barnum Brown, the paleontologist who had described *Saurolophus* four years earlier. The two dinosaurs may not have been as closely related as their names suggest. New research in 2004 linked *Prosaurolophus* more closely to *Gryposaurus*. A bonebed discovered in Montana suggests that *Prosaurolophus* sometimes lived together. Scientists think these creatures may have gathered by a water source during a time of drought. In general, though, the fossil record in Alberta showed that *Prosaurolophus* lived in a warm climate, with wet and dry seasons.

DINOSAUR

LATE CRETACEOUS

Prosaurolophus was a large-headed duckbill. Its beak was perfect for clipping the flowering plants, shrubs, and fruits it ate. The back of its mouth was filled with thousands of teeth for grinding up food.

Crest
Above its eyes was a small triangular crest, which may have helped to tell different creatures (or males and females) apart.

WHERE IN THE WORLD?

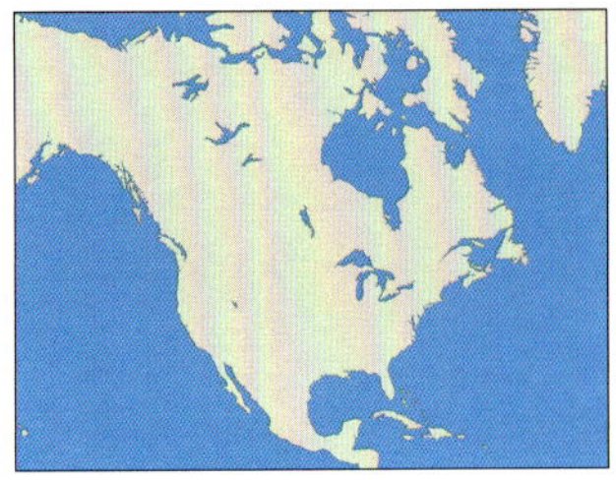

Prosaurolophus was located in Alberta, Canada, and Montana.

HOW BIG IS IT?

Hind Legs
Though it walked on all fours, *Prosaurolophus* could probably get up onto its hind legs, resting against its tail for balance.

TIMELINE (millions of years ago)

540 | 505 | 438 | 408 | 360 | 280 | 248 | 208 | 146 | 65 | 1.8 to today

Parasaurolophus

• **ORDER** • Ornithischia • **FAMILY** • Hadrosauridae
• **GENUS & SPECIES** • Several species within the genus *Parasaurolophus*

This hadrosaur had a fancy crest curving from the back of its head that may have helped it communicate to others and could have acted as a volume control for its calls.

VITAL STATISTICS

Fossil Location	North America
Diet	Herbivorous
Pronunciation	Pah-ra-SAWR-ro-lo-fous
Weight	2.7 tons (2.5 tonnes)
Length	13 ft (9.5 m)
Height	15 ft (4.9 m)
Meaning of Name	"Near *Saurolophus*" since it was thought to be a very close relative of that dinosaur

FOSSIL EVIDENCE

The crest ranges in size between specimens. At its longest it forms a curved hollow tube 6 ft (1.8 m) long. *Parasaurolophus* has been called the "trumpet dinosaur" because its crest could have increased the volume of the sounds it made when communicating. Or the crest may just have been a special feature to help others recognize it. The large eye sockets are a sign that *Parasaurolophus* had sharp vision and may have been active at dusk. Fossilized stomach contents show that it ate land plants, even though scientists once thought that it lived mainly in water.

DINOSAUR

LATE CRETACEOUS

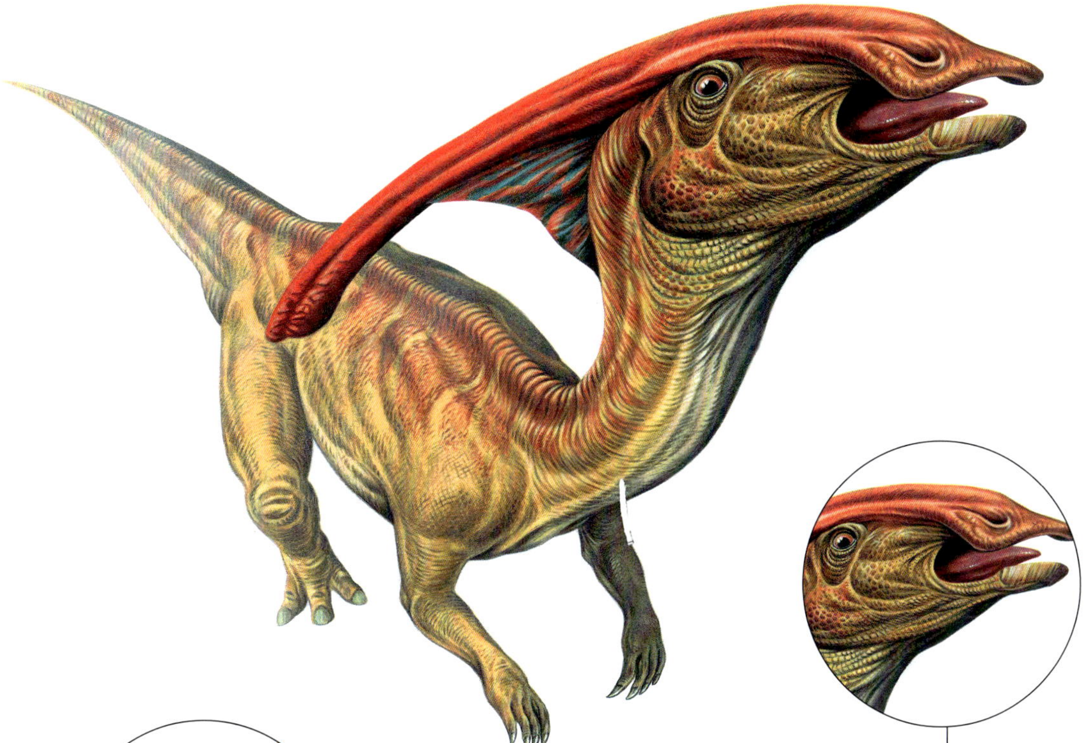

Jaw
The jaw was built to allow the numerous cheek teeth to make a grinding motion in order to chew.

Notch
The tip of the crest may have set into a notch in the backbone but the purpose of this feature is entirely unknown.

HOW BIG IS IT?

WHERE IN THE WORLD?

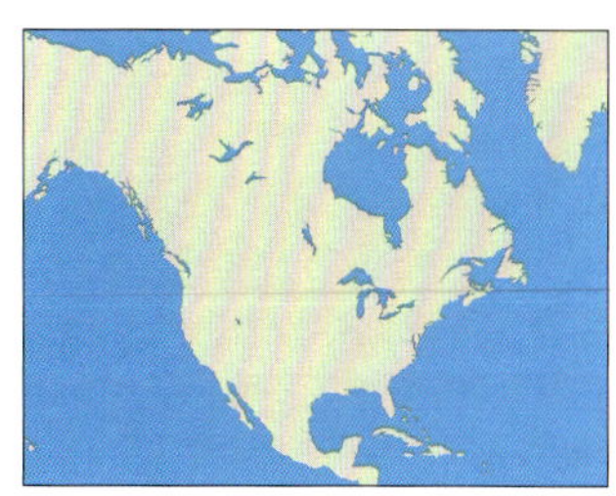

First dug up in Alberta, Canada, later findings were discovered in New Mexico and Utah.

TIMELINE (millions of years ago)

540 | 505 | 438 | 408 | 360 | 280 | 248 | 208 | 146 | 65 | 1.8 to today

Protoceratops

VITAL STATISTICS

Fossil Location	Mongolia and China
Diet	Herbivorous
Pronunciation	Proh-toh-SEH-ratops
Weight	400 lb (181 kg)
Length	6 ft (1.8 m)
Height	2 ft (0.6 m)
Meaning of Name	"First horn face" because it was first thought to be an ancestor (early relative) of later horned dinosaurs

FOSSIL EVIDENCE
The first *Protoceratops* find was made in 1922 in the Gobi Desert of Mongolia by a photographer, J.B. Shackleford. Shackleford belonged to a United States expedition exploring the desert in search of the ancestors (early relatives) of humans. The *Protoceratops* fossils were very well preserved. In 1971, an important find was made of a double fossil showing a *Protoceratops* fighting with a *Velociraptor*. It seems that the two dinosaurs died together, possibly in a mudslide,

DINOSAUR

LATE CRETACEOUS

Protoceratops had a large bony frill around its neck. Some think the frill was to protect _Protoceratops_'s neck and add strength to its jaw muscles, but it was probably too delicate to help much with those jobs. The muscles had plenty of work to do because, like most other herbivores, _Protoceratops_ ate tons of vegetation. Although it was fairly long, measuring up to 6 ft (1.8 m), _Protoceratops_ was pretty low to the ground, only 2 ft (0.6 m) in height. Its body was shaped like a barrel, and it had a short tail, short legs with five-toed feet, and birdlike hips.

WHERE IN THE WORLD?

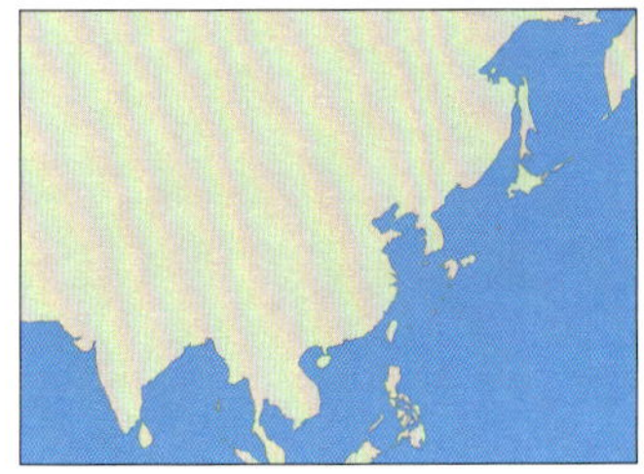

Protoceratops has been found in Gansu and in the Bayan Mandahu Formation of Mongolia.

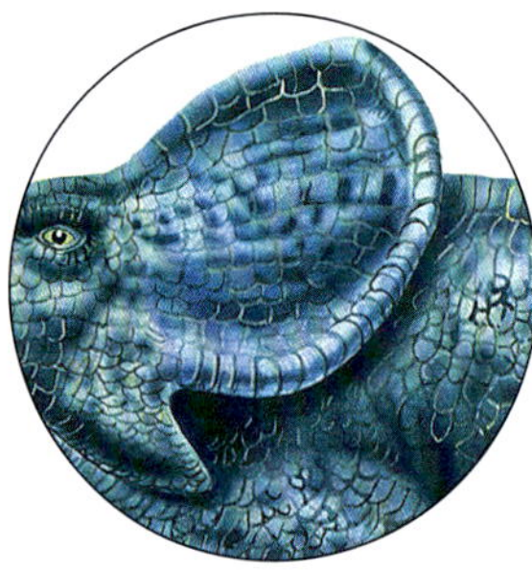

Frill
Scientists do not know what the frill did, but it probably helped with species recognition. (Friends and enemies could tell what species this creature was by seeing the frill.)

• **ORDER** • Ornithischia • **FAMILY** • Protoceratopsidae • **GENUS & SPECIES** • *Protoceratops andrewsi, P. hellenikorhinus*

FANCY FRILLS
Protoceratops's head frills were strong enough to survive millions of years after its death. The fossils show the curious eaglelike look its bony mask gave to its face. In *Protoceratops andrewsi* there were two forms of frills. One type was bigger than the other and is a sign that there might have been differences in the frills of males and females.

HERDING ANIMAL
Protoceratops may have been a herding animal, and paleontologists have called it "the sheep of the Cretaceous" because its fossils are so common in the Gobi Desert.

HOW BIG IS IT?

TIMELINE (millions of years ago)

540 | 505 | 438 | 408 | 360 | 280 | 248 | 208 | 146 | 65 | 1.8 to today

Protoceratops

• **ORDER** • Ornithischia • **FAMILY** • Protoceratopsidae • **GENUS & SPECIES** • *Protoceratops andrewsi, P. hellenikorhinus*

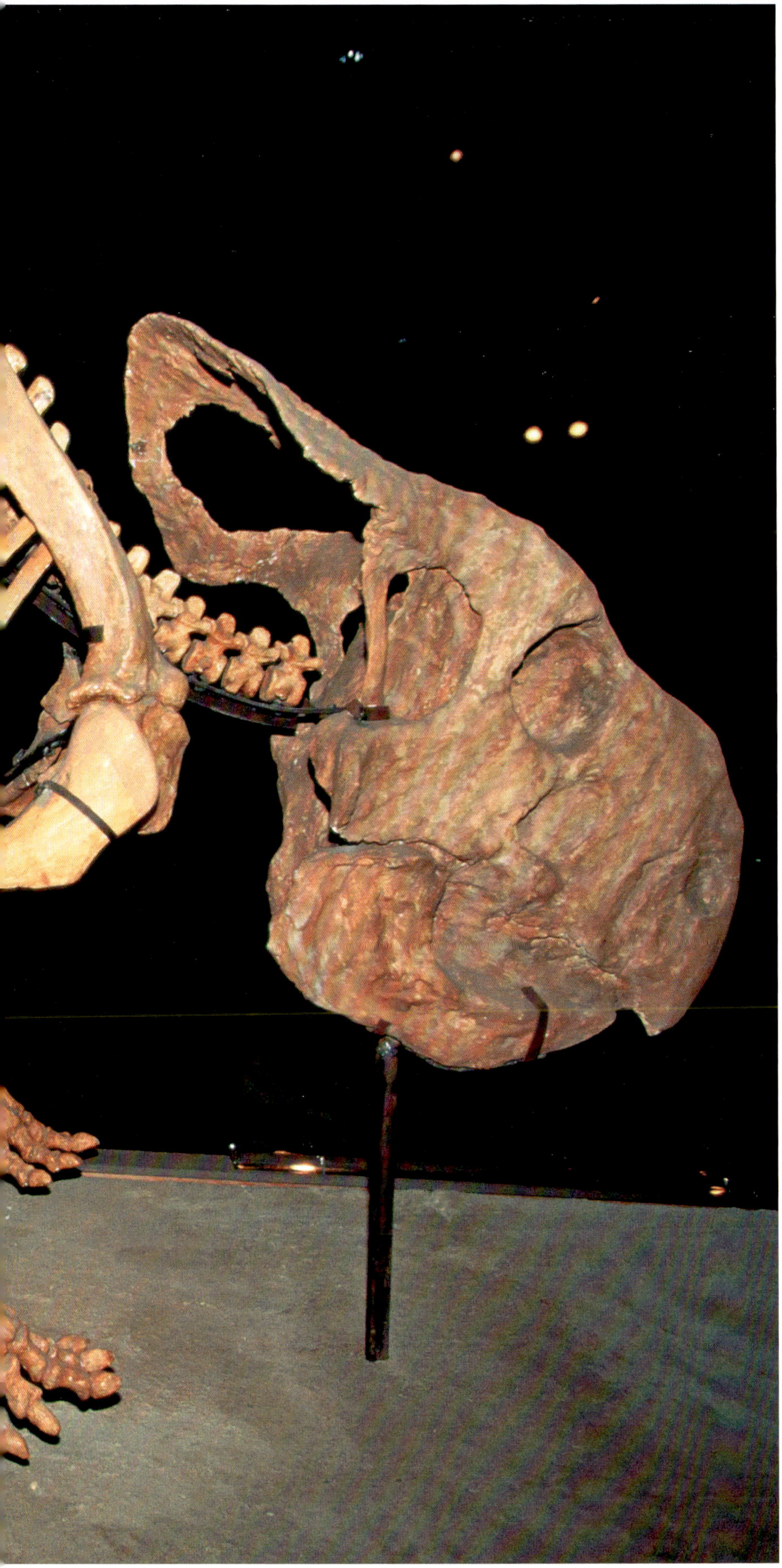

GRIFFIN OR PROTOCERATOPS?

The griffin was a pretend creature from mythology that was supposed to have an eagle's head and wings. It was also said to have the body of a lion and lay its eggs in nests on the ground. But, more than 2,600 years ago, in 675 BCE, Ancient Greek writers wrote about the discovery of griffins as if they were real-life creatures. The Ancient Greek writers may have heard about the griffins from nomads (traveling people who move from place to place). A group of nomads were mining for gold in Central Asia. In red sandstone, they may have come across fossil skeletons and other remains. These nomads told the Ancient Greeks about the creatures they had uncovered, and then the Greeks wrote about those creatures. Their descriptions match the descriptions of *Protoceratops* that paleontologists made hundreds of years later. The nomads may have made up the griffin myth to explain the fossils they found, and the Ancient Greeks thought they were writing about real-life creatures. In fact, it seems like the gold-hunting nomads and the Ancient Greeks may have been talking about the fossil remains of *Protoceratops*. In China and Mongolia, where many *Protoceratops* fossils have been found, gold has been found, too. So the clues do add up!

Triceratops

VITAL STATISTICS

Fossil Location	North America
Diet	Herbivorous
Pronunciation	Try-SER-a-tops
Weight	26,455 lb (12,000 kg)
Length	29 ft 6 in (9 m)
Height	10 ft (3 m)
Meaning of name	"Three-horned face"

FOSSIL EVIDENCE

The first *Triceratops* find of 1877 was sent to Othniel Charles Marsh, the famous paleontologist. He thought it came from the Pliocene period, 5.3–1.8 million years ago. Marsh also mistakenly thought that the remains had been a type of bison that he called *Bison alticornis*. He changed his mind in 1888, though, after examining two more skulls. These convinced him that what he had thought was a bison was actually a dinosaur.

DINOSAUR

LATE CRETACEOUS

Triceratops **is one of the most famous dinosaurs. Hundreds of** ***Triceratops*** **skulls and other remains have been found, with the Hell Creek Formation in Montana providing an especially large number of finds.** ***Triceratops*** **skulls were very rugged, which helps explains why they have survived so well for 72 million years.**

WHERE IN THE WORLD?

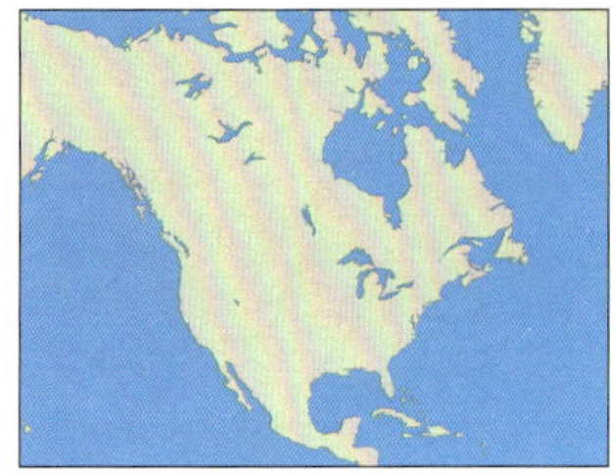

Triceratops has been found in Colorado, Wyoming, Montana, and South Dakota and in Alberta and Saskatchewan in Canada.

Horns
Triceratops's three sharp horns might have been used to scare predators but were also important in species recognition.

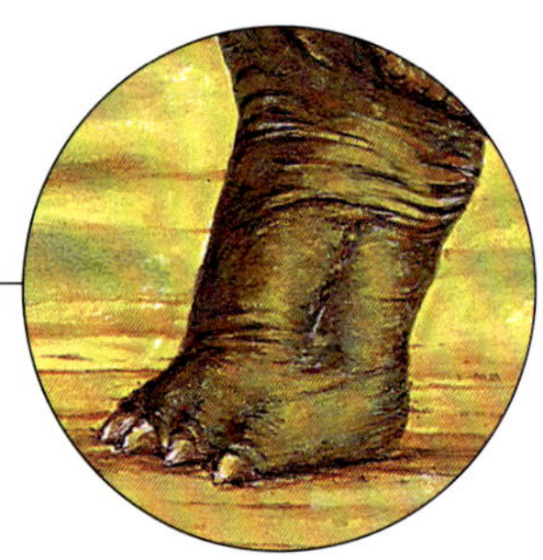

Legs
Triceratops had huge chunky legs that supported its heavy bulk.

• **ORDER** • Ornithischia • **FAMILY** • Ceratopsidae • **GENUS & SPECIES** • *Triceratops horridus, T. prorsus*

IDENTIFYING MALES AND FEMALES

In 1986, more than a century after *Triceratops* was first discovered, the American paleontologist Thomas M. Lehman suggested that male and female examples of this dinosaur could be identified by their skulls and horns. Lehman thought that the males had larger skulls and more upright horns. They were taller than the female *Triceratops*, who had shorter horns that leaned forward.

Triceratops was not among the largest herbivores, but it was tough and was likely a fierce opponent when threatened or attacked.

TEETH IN RESERVE

The teeth of *Triceratops* lined its mouth in batteries. Up to 40 columns of teeth grew on each side of its jaw, with around five teeth stacked in each column. This meant that *Triceratops* had some 432 teeth in all, and if any of them were damaged or broken, another would grow in its place. This arrangement of teeth would have made it easy for *Triceratops* to eat large amounts of tough, fibrous plants such as cycads, palms, or ferns.

HOW BIG IS IT?

TIMELINE (millions of years ago)

540	505	438	408	360	280	248	208	146	65	1.8 to today

Triceratops

• **ORDER** • Ornithischia • **FAMILY** • Ceratopsidae • **GENUS & SPECIES** • *Triceratops horridus, T. prorsus*

LOTS OF FINDS

Triceratops fossils are among the most frequently found non-avian (not birdlike) dinosaurs known. This is probably testimony to their great abundance in the Late Cretaceous since, even though bone beds of *Triceratops* are uncommon, most finds are of single individuals. Despite this, *Triceratops* finds have been so prolific that one paleontologist, Bruce Erickson of the Science Museum of Minnesota, observed around 200 examples of *Triceratops prorsus*, which was first discovered in 1890 by Charles Othniel Marsh in the Hell Creek Formation in Montana. Another paleontologist, Barnum Brown, did even better. He claimed to have seen more than 500 skulls in the same area. In the west of North America, hundreds of fragments of *Triceratops* teeth, horns, frills, and other pieces of skull have been discovered, leading to the conclusion that *Triceratops* was one of the most common herbivores of the Late Cretaceous. Some paleontologists go further and class this dinosaur as the most dominant of its time. American paleontologist Robert Bakker reckoned in 1986 that *Triceratops* accounted for more than 80 percent of all large dinosaurs at the end of the Cretaceous Period.

Styracosaurus

• **ORDER** • Ornithischia • **FAMILY** • Ceratopsidae • **GENUS & SPECIES** • *Styracosaurus albertensis*

VITAL STATISTICS

Fossil Location	North America
Diet	Herbivorous
Pronunciation	Styra-co-SAWR-us
Weight	6,613 lb (3,000 kg)
Length	18 ft (5.5 m)
Height	6 ft (1.8 m)
Meaning of name	"Spiked lizard"

FOSSIL EVIDENCE
Styracosaurus was a large, horned, and frilled dinosaur with a body resembling that of a rhinoceros. The first *Styracosaurus* fossils (parts of a skull and skeleton) were discovered in 1913 in Alberta, Canada, in the area now named Dinosaur Park Formation. Later finds, such as the lower jaws and the remainder of the skeleton, were made in 1935. In 1915, a US expedition uncovered a nearly complete skeleton with part of its skull, also in the Dinosaur Park. Further discoveries were made in 2006.

DINOSAUR

LATE CRETACEOUS

Styracosaurus's terrifying appearance probably deterred attackers but was also likely used for species recognition. Its head was adorned with several long, barbarous-looking spikes and its nose had a fearsome protruding horn.

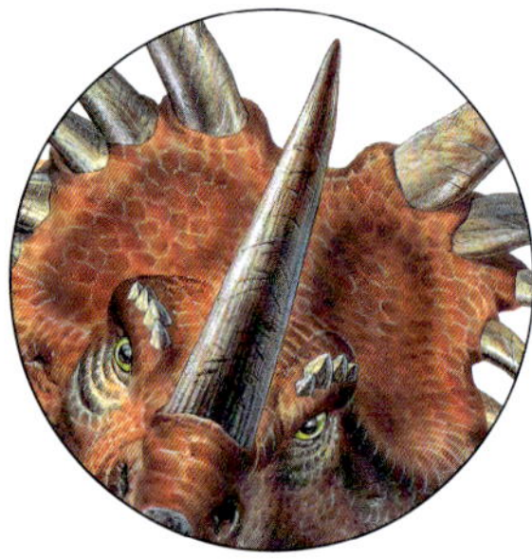

Nose Horn
The long horn on the center of *Styracosaurus's* nose measured 22 in (57 cm) in length in the fossilized skull but was even longer in the living animal because of the keratin sheath that it would have had over the bone.

WHERE IN THE WORLD?

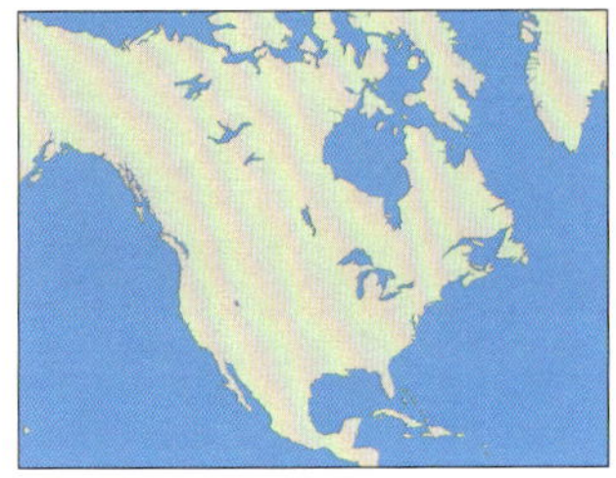

Styracosaurus remains were found in Montana and Wyoming and at the Judith River Group in Alberta, Canada.

HOW BIG IS IT?

Beak
Styracosaurus's sharply pointed beak, used for snapping off vegetation.

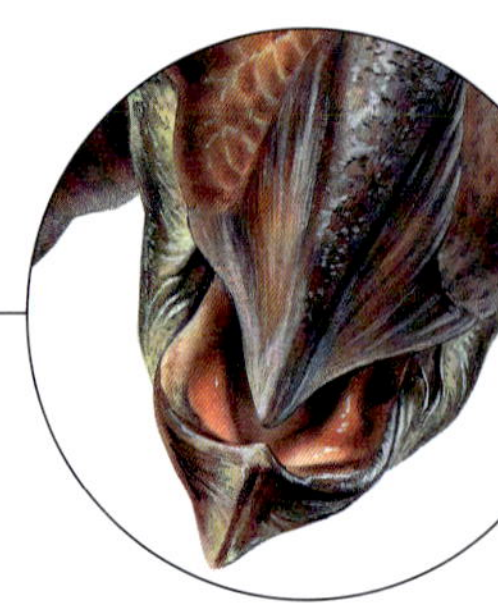

TIMELINE (millions of years ago)

540	505	438	408	360	280	248	208	146	65	1.8 to today

Glossary

avian (AY-vee-an) Having to do with birds

biodiversity (by-oh-dih-VER-sih-tee) When an environment contains many different types of plants and animals

copious (KO-pee-us) Plentiful; a large quantity

cranium (KRAY-nee-um) A part of the skull that contains the brain

drought (JROWT) A period of time with little or no rain

estuaries (ES-chuw-air-ez) Water passages where a larger sea meets a river

fossil (FAH-sil) Remains or traces of an organism from the past that have been preserved, such as bones, teeth, footprints, etc.

mandible (MAN-dih-bul) A jawbone

paleontologist (pay-lee-on-TAH-luh-jist) A scientist who studies fossils

photosynthesis (foh-toh-SIN-thih-sis) Process by which plants convert sunlight into food

radiate (RAY-dee-ayt) To spread out from the center

scavenger (SKA-vin-jer) Animals that usually do not kill their own food, but feed on the carcasses left behind by other predators

shale (SHAYL) Layered rock made up of a combination of mud, clay, or silt

swath (SWAHTH) A long, broad strip

Index

For More Information

Books

Sheldon, David. *Barnum Brown: Dinosaur Hunter.* New York: Walker Books for Young Readers, 2006.

Shone, Rob. *Triceratops: The Three Horned Dinosaur.* New York: PowerKids Press, 2007.

Williams, Judith. *The Discovery and Mystery of a Dinosaur Named Jane.* Berkeley Heights, NJ: Enslow Publishers, 2007.

Web Sites

To ensure the currency and safety of recommended Internet links, Windmill maintains and updates an online list of sites related to the subject of this book. To access this list of Web sites, please go to www.windmillbooks.com/weblinks and select this book's title.